C000001027

Frontispiece A corner of the carpet section of the Aq Chah Bazaar. Courtesy Dr. Elmor Rigamor

ORIENTAL RUGS

Volume 3

The Carpets of Afghanistan

To

Stephanie Crockett

with best wishes

from

Richard Parsons

Hong Kong
15-12-93

ORIENTAL RUGS

Volume 3

The Carpets of Afghanistan

R.D. Parsons

Antique Collectors' Club

© 1983 R.D. Parsons

World copyright reserved

First published 1983
New edition 1987
New edition 1990

All rights reserved. No part of this publication may be reproduced, stored in a retrieval system or transmitted in any form or by any means electronic, mechanical, photocopying, recording or otherwise, without the prior permission of the publishers.

British Library CIP Data

Oriental rugs.
   Vol. 3: The carpets of Afghanistan. 3rd rev. ed.
   1 Asian rugs
   I. Parsons, Richard D.
   746.7581

ISBN 1 85149 144 9

Published for the Antique Collectors' Club
by the Antique Collectors' Club Ltd.

Printed in England by Antique Collectors' Club Ltd., Woodbridge, Suffolk

This book is dedicated to Mohamad Yassin
and all my Afghan friends wherever they may be . . . .

Acknowledgements

No book such as this is the work of one person alone. To all who have made their contribution whether by answering numerous and searching questions, accompanying me on long and arduous journeys, acting as guide or interpreter, typing manuscripts, reading through and criticising drafts, my grateful thanks. I wish to mention specifically Sayeed Mustapha Hashemi, my devoted friend and colleague; Carla Grissmann for her unstinting help and critical advice with the early drafts; Dr. Louis Dupree and his wife, Nancy Hatch Dupree, for their valuable comments and unfailing encouragement, also for the use of some of their slides which appear as black and white photographs; Bryan M. Huffner for his objective criticisms and his much appreciated suggestions — also for putting so many of his company's resources at my disposal, especially carpets from stock for photography; Robert Tate who took so many photographs of carpets in Kabul, a number of which appear in this book; Dr. D.M. Lewis of the IWS for his contribution in connection with the chemistry of ashqar.

I am very grateful to Mr. P. Van Aalst, Mr. Bohmler, Mr. Engelhardt, Dr. Elmor Rigamor, and to Josephine Powell for their photographs, which are acknowledged in the captions to the relevant photographs, also to Richard Ringrose, some of whose transparencies are included among the black and white photographs; last, but by no means least, to Patrick Burke, who took the majority of the photographs which appear in this book.

My very deep gratitude to Carla Grissman for her invaluable help, encouragement and hospitality during the period when I was writing the additional material which appears in this revised edition.

I also wish to express my sincere thanks to Shir Khosrow Paiwand whose superb collection of old Beluch rugs he so generously placed at my disposal.

Contents

Colour Plates

Publisher's Note

This revised edition contains forty extra colour plates and two new chapters. With the exception of new plates 114-124, which appear in these two chapters, the additional colour is placed in appropriate sections throughout the book and carries a number followed by the letter 'a', 'b' or 'c'.

Foreword

In the summer of 1979, the Government of Afghanistan issued a decree which virtually restricted foreign residents from travelling within the country. At the time of this announcement, I was in the middle of a twenty-five day tour of the western part of Afghanistan, better acquainting myself with some of the more remote and scattered villages in which tribal rugs of the Beluch type are made. Little did I think, when embarking on this tour from Kabul — my home for the previous seven years — that this would be my last trip to the carpet producing areas of Afghanistan! To me personally, this ban on travel was a sad and severe blow. Not only was my work as a carpet buyer restricted, but it also marked the end of my friendship and contacts with so many people of different clans, tribes and ethnic groups which make up the population of this magnificent country. Afghanistan may be economically poor and technologically backward, yet it is rich in culture and scenic beauty. Its people, very independent and proudly individualistic, are secure in the religion of their forefathers. As yet they are unaffected by the shoddiness and superficiality of twentieth-century Western 'civilisation'. The age-old standards of true hospitality are rigidly adhered to, as are all the codes of conduct which have evolved over countless generations in a land fraught with the rigours and harshness of the elements, extremes of temperatures, periodic droughts, sand storms, and the ravages of disease. Thus it was that, on my return to Kabul, I decided to write this book, a record of the carpets of Afghanistan in the context of the people who weave them, and of the places in which they are woven.

Those who seek a work of erudite scholarship will be disappointed, for this book is aimed at sharing my love of Afghanistan and its carpets with as many people as possible and especially with owners and would-be owners of a rug from Afghanistan. I have, therefore, deliberately kept descriptive technicalities to a minimum for, rightly or wrongly, I consider that someone who enjoys his Afghan rug and who has been able to identify its provenance with the help of this book, will not feel unduly let down by not being told that, for instance, the yarn of a particular piece was Z rather than S plied!

In all forms of arts and crafts there is a constant evolution, sometimes barely perceptible, at other times more marked. Were it not so, that particular art form would die. Afghan carpets are no exception to this rule, and I would stress that what is chronicled in this book is a true and fair record of the Afghan carpet industry as at the time of writing. Over the years many changes have taken place, of which some are commented on herein. As time goes by, other changes will take place, both as regards construction and execution of design, and this book will have to be amended. One of my fondest dreams is that circumstances may allow me to do this!

However, if this is not to be, then I fervently hope that some other lover of Afghanistan and its carpets will unhesitatingly undertake the task. I believe that, during these times of turbulent happenings and changes in so many traditional carpet-producing countries — and bearing in mind that both India and Egypt are now producing excellent copies of Persian carpets — it is important to record changes, be they evolutionary or tending towards a renaissance, for the benefit of future generations.

Let us now look at some of the reasons for these changes which have already taken place in the Afghan carpet production. Firstly, intermarriage between clans and even tribes is now far more frequent than it was some two decades ago. Thus, when a Turkoman of, say, the Karaboiin sub-clan marries a Taghan wife, she may well introduce one or more motifs from her own clan into the Karaboiin design. The other womenfolk in the compound, liking this innovation introduced by the young bride, may start copying this deviation from tradition — and so a hybrid is born! Secondly, the opening up of the country and better communications have resulted in certain hitherto remote communities becoming far more accessible and susceptible to external influences — not least of which is the itinerant trader. These new influences have resulted in a further mixture of motifs, and in some cases certain clans have totally abandoned their own traditional designs in favour of 'what everyone else is making'.

Yet a third reason for change is due to the commercialisation of the Afghan production. As demand has increased so have the less attractive aspects of commercialism — some of which are directed towards the getting of a piece off the loom as quickly as possible. This inevitably leads to cutting corners and to simplification. In the case of designs, this is sometimes achieved by the enlarging of certain motifs at the expense of eliminating others. The old flat selvedge made from goats' or horses' hair has been largely replaced by a blanket-stitch binding, whilst skilled methods of indigo vat dyeing are being supplanted by the use of 'instant' blue from a tin.

However, not all changes have been for the worse. There is no doubt that in several weaving areas the standard of carpet production has improved considerably. For instance, it is becoming increasingly difficult to differentiate between the modern Alti Bolaq — traditionally a very good quality — and the Andkhoy production. The resuscitation of old designs and the increased use of natural dyestuffs in certain areas are other examples of changes for the better.

The whole of the Afghan carpet production — i.e. The Turkoman as well as both the Beluch and Beluch-type — is a tribal one, and the good pieces may be likened to a flower in an old-fashioned garden. Beautiful in itself, it will enhance its surroundings at the same time as blending in with them. Certainly, a distinctive feature of these pieces is that the bold, rectilinear patterns complemented by subtle yet simple border motifs, the whole well executed in good yarn with harmonious colours, look equally imposing in the classical chateau as in the Elizabethan timber-framed house — or, indeed, in the characteristic, utilitarian concrete and glass edifices which dominate so many of today's towns and cities.

The very fact that this production is a tribal one often makes it very difficult to pin-point accurately the exact place where a particular rug was made.

In the case of nomads and transhumants, they will be in different places according to the time of year. Where the Ersaris are concerned, most sub-clans of this Turkoman majority group live in scattered settlements often bearing the name of the clan which is numerically superior. Hence it is often the case that one can have a Taghan rug woven in the village of Chakesh and vice versa.

An additional source of confusion is that in the trade certain qualities and/or designs have been allocated names of places which bear no relation to the actual origin of the piece, and the reader would be well advised not to draw conclusions from trade names such as 'Daulatabad', 'Maimana' etc.

In a tribal production such as is found in Afghanistan, where yarn is hand spun, the knot count of any given piece should never be equated with quality. The combination of colour, design and material is far more important than the *number* of knots in a given area. This does not mean that the *standard* of knotting is unimportant, for obviously the regularity and tightness, or density, of the fabric are important factors, yet one cannot ignore the fact that in the last analysis it is the yarn count of the warp, weft and pile which very largely predetermines the knot count.

I am frequently asked whether the purchase of an Afghan rug is a good investment, to which I invariably reply in the affirmative. Of course, much depends on what is meant by 'investment' and whether it is intended to realise it. One must assume that a rug or carpet which is enjoyed by its owner will not normally be sold and, therefore, for a modest outlay one can acquire a source of constant pleasure. In spite of inflationary tendencies, it is interesting to note that over the last thirty years or so, the wholesale price of new Afghan goods has increased by only about twelvefold, and in the case of semi-antique goods, the increase has been in the order of twentyfold over a similar period. However, quite apart from fluctuating exchange rates, imposition of taxes, etc., it is always unsafe to refer to prices, especially as these usually increase at different stages of progress before reaching the retailer's shop, and every time there is a change of ownership thereafter. One of these stages through which a large part of the Afghan production goes is the chemical washing, of which there are various kinds, some of which are very expensive. This in effect is a 'packaging' deal designed to make the raw piece straight from the loom more attractive and, therefore, more saleable. There are different chemical washes which give results varying from an artificial sheen to a wash which tones down bright colours — or even transforms them radically. (In this context it should be noted that practically all the pieces photographed in this book are of untreated/unwashed pieces). The object of these washes is to produce an effect similar in appearance to that which would result by the natural processes of fair wear and tear. Good yarn soon develops a natural sheen with use and brushing, whilst normal exposure to sunlight will result in oxidation of dyestuffs. Natural dyestuffs oxidise rapidly and result sooner in that softness of tones which is so much sought after in older goods.

However, in our appreciation of semi-antique pieces, let us not forget that they started off by being very new!

There are very few — if any — Afghan rugs which can be certified as antiques — i.e. as being more than one hundred years old. The term 'semi-antique' as used in this book describes a piece which has attained a respectable age, generally not less than some forty years or so, but still somewhat short of a century! When suggesting an age, I have been cautious not to exaggerate and may well have erred on the conservative side.

By the description 'oldish' is meant a piece which may look older than it is. This applies particularly to Beluch and Beluch-type production from which pieces are quite often found whose dyestuffs have oxidised especially quickly and have thus assumed a mellowness associated with age. In other words, an 'oldish piece' is one that often looks older than it is, and generally could be anything from five to twenty-five years old.

The term 'used' or *zir-i-pai* signifies a piece which, through use, has lost much of the newness or 'rawness' associated with pieces which come straight off the loom. Such pieces would probably be no more than three to five years old. In accordance with common usage in Afghanistan, throughout this book I have used the term *kilim* to mean any pileless weave or pileless fabric, regardless of its technical construction, and all flat-woven ends of carpets and rugs. All measurements refer to the piled area only and, where appropriate, the lengths of the *kilims* are stated separately.

Introduction

Ten years ago when I wrote the foreword to the first edition of *The Carpets of Afghanistan,* I stated that this book would have to be amended in order to include such changes in production, construction and designs as would inevitably take place.

Little did I anticipate the intensity of fighting, the scale of destruction, or the heart-rending social upheavels that Afghanistan and its people were to suffer. Since December, 1979, when the Soviet Union invaded Afghanistan, over one million Afghans have been killed; more than five million have fled to Pakistan, Iran and Turkey and elsewhere; one million are internally displaced refugees within their own country. This adds up to over half the population of Afghanistan, either killed or having fled their homes and living in exile.

It should not be assumed that merely because the Soviet army has withdrawn from Afghanistan, conditions will soon return to normal. The entire infrastructure of the country has suffered. Vast areas are seeded with millions of mines, irrigation systems have been destroyed, as have roads, agricultural lands, forests, livestock. The Agricultural Survey of Afghanistan, carried out under the auspices of the Swedish Committee for Afghanistan, estimate that the flocks of Karaqul sheep have been reduced by at least fifty percent. No aspect of life has been left unscathed, and the task of rebuilding Afghanistan is of a magnitude unprecedented in history.

I have been fortunate in being able to maintain contact with many Afghan families and friends, both amongst those who remained in Afghanistan and those who are living as refugees in Pakistan and Turkey. Furthermore, having established an oriental carpet trading company in south-east Asia, in conjunction with two valued Afghan friends, one of whom — Haji Sayed Mustapha — continues to send me regular shipments of prime-quality Afghan goods, I have been able to keep in close touch with events in Afghanistan, as well as with developments in its carpet industry.

In spite of the war, the production in carpets in Afghanistan has continued, albeit hampered by periodic shortages of wool, due to the depletion of flocks through drought, slaughter for food or as a result of enemy action. What is remarkable is that despite all the upheavels and suffering, some totally new productions have been created and are being sold in the open market!

Many of the traditional weavers, as well as newly trained ones, living in various refugee camps in Pakistan, Iran and Turkey, have also been making carpets. However, in the context of the traditional Afghan carpet (both Turkoman and Beluch) a significant proportion of these productions has deviated from the accepted and classical criteria, primarily in materials used, but also in designs.

In the following pages I have divided these issues into two main parts: the changes within Afghanistan and the production made by Afghan refugees. Whilst it has been impossible to quantify the changes which have taken place, or the tribal groupings and their current locations, every effort has been made to present an accurate description of developments in the art of carpet weaving both within Afghanistan and the refugee camps wherever they may be.

It may well be another decade before these are consolidated!

Peshawar
July 1989

Chapter 1

The Gateway to Afghan Turkestan

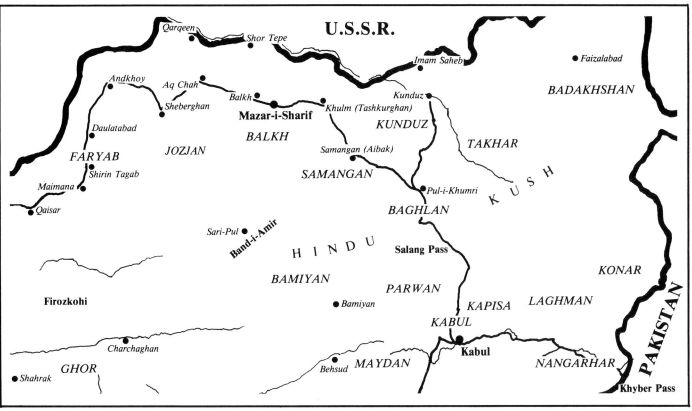

The paved road from Kabul to Mazar-i-Sharif was completed in 1964, before which time the northern and southern parts of Afghanistan were cut off from each other during the long winter months when snow lay thick over the Hindu Kush. Crossing the Salang Pass, at 3,363 metres the highest macadamised road in Afghanistan, the scenery is of awesome splendour. The stark, grey-brown ruggedness of the mountains is relieved by bright patches of small, cultivated valleys with scattered plantations of poplars. Afghanistan, a country of mountains and deserts, is a man's country, yet its very harshness, grandeur and serenity bring a man down to his proper level.

Some two hundred and fifty kilometres north of Kabul one reaches the town of Pul-i-Khumri (the Bridge of the Doves), near which wild pistachio trees grow in abundance. Here the road divides: the right fork leads to the major provincial capital of Kunduz and thence through Faizalabad and on to the remote Wakhan Corridor and the Pamir mountains, the home of the Marco Polo sheep. Taking the left fork one crosses the fertile plain on the far side of Pul-i-Khumri, whose major crops are rice and sugar beet, which has a

Badakhshan on the way to the Pamirs

A Turkoman oven in which their flattish round loaves are baked; the dough is stuck on to the oven walls

markedly different atmosphere, and the traveller feels himself approaching that fascinating region of Afghan Turkestan.

Perhaps part of this fascination is due to the large numbers of horses grazing along the sides of the road, for Samangan, or Aibak as it is also called, is a famous centre for the breeding of dray and hack horses. It is here that one finds for the first time kababs worthy of the name, those pieces of mutton interspersed with the special fat from the sheep's tail grilled on a skewer over charcoal and seasoned with red pepper and crushed grape pips. The whole is eaten with hot, fresh unleavened Uzbek brown bread and sliced raw onions, washed down with green tea. Samangan is also famous for its fourth-century Buddhist stupa and monastery carved out of the living rock. The sacred lotus blossom is still discernible on the ceiling ten metres above one's head.

A few kilometres further on, in the village of Old Aibak, live Arabis, people of Arab descent though now calling themselves Uzbeks, who with Uzbeks practise the ancient craft of metal casting. They work in individual compounds, each specialising in a particular item. In one are cast axles for the *gaadi,* the local two-wheeled cart for the transportation of people and light loads; in another are cast the huge cauldrons used in the tea houses for cooking rice, or by dyers for their vats. The metal comes from broken-down gear-boxes and other parts of those lorries which are beyond the repairing skill of even the most ingenious Afghan mechanic, who has no mean reputation for keeping derelict vehicles on the road.

In the dark interiors of the workshops, two men arduously turn a five-foot wheel which operates a large goatskin bellows directed into the charcoal fire; the heat is terrific and able to render a crankshaft into molten metal in less than an hour. The results obtained from the skill with which these craftsmen use totally unsophisticated equipment are extraordinary.

Samangan is a traditional centre for the weaving of *kilims* (in Afghanistan, usually pronounced *gilam*) but not of piled goods. Alas, the Samangan *kilims,* made by the Uzbek and Arabi of the area, are a thing of the past, though odd pieces still sometimes appear on the market. Like most *kilims,* they tend to be long and narrow, woven in one piece or in bands later sewn together, using both 'tapestry slit-weave' and 'loose-weft' techniques. A full range of bright colours was used. (See Colour Plates 1, 2, 3 and 4). Current woven production from this area is small, comprising trappings for horses, narrow decorative tent bands, saddle clothes and horse blankets.

Tashkurghan, also called Khulm, some seventy-five kilometres north of Samangan, lies in a fertile oasis of fruit trees watered by mountain streams. The population of Tashkurghan includes Tajiks and Pashtuns, but no Turkomans, who are found further north. Tashkurghan is renowned for its scenic beauty, its figs and pomegranates, and the fact that it has the oldest and one of the few remaining covered bazaars in Afghanistan. The town, approached from the south through a narrow gorge, spreads along the foothills of the Tashkurghan Range, nestled against a spectacular stone backdrop of red, brown, pale olive green, fawn and purple, ever changing as the sun moves across the sky.

The main bazaar of Tashkurghan is built of mud brick and is an excellent example of Islamic domestic architecture. The dome of the central market is decorated with stalactites and inlaid with cups and saucers of Chinese porcelain dating to 1845. Of interest is the fact that the inner wall of this little court is twelve-sided, whilst the outer wall is sixteen-sided, so that the inner and outer facets of both polygons are the same length. Consequently, all the shops are of the same size. Other bazaar streets lead off from this small central enclosure but their walls are of clay, having poplar beams covered with woven reed mats for the roof.

Craftsmen and merchants sell all kinds of haberdashery, cloth, and Hong

The gorge on the outskirts of Tashkurghan

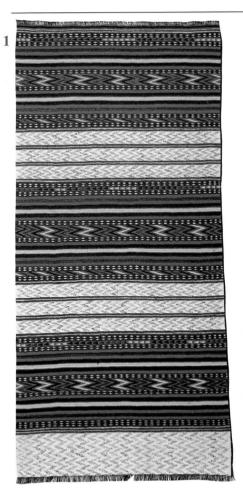

1

2

4

Colour Plate 2 A fine and gaily coloured UZBEK KILIM. A typical example of this type which is woven in narrow bands which are then sewn together. Hence, these pieces are seldom symmetrical. The finest Karaqul wool is used. Alas, another example of a type which, whilst still available, is no longer being made.

Courtesy Josephine Powell

Colour Plate 1 UZBEK KILIM marketed in Aibak (Samangan) and most probably made in the area. The wool is not Karaqul; probably Ghilzai. This type of kilim *is still obtainable, but is no longer being made. (188 x 89cm).*

3

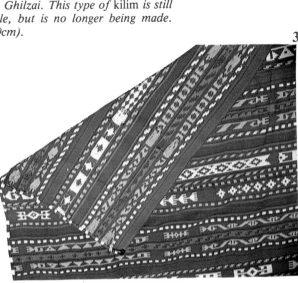

Colour Plate 3 A fine ARABI KILIM. This fine fabric is often called a ghajari. (331 x 193cm).

Colour Plate 4 A coarse ARABI KILIM. (200 x 102cm).

5

Colour Plate 5 An UZBEK KILIM bag from Tashkurghan. Note the brown woollen fringes are not from Karaqul wool. Both colouring and design are very reminiscent of Kirghiz bags, a few of which are still in the possession of the Kirghiz tribes which lived in the Pamirs until they fled to the Gilgit and Hunza Valleys of the North West Frontier Province of Pakistan, where they are now settled. (68 x 57cm).

Colour Plate 6 A BUZKASHI whip. The handle is decorated with silver bands.
Author's collection

6

Kong, Korea and Taiwan products of plastic and metal. Silversmiths and goldsmiths sit cross-legged, toiling over the ornaments intended for the brides and wives, while an apprentice diligently operates the bellows. Leather workers make shoes, riding boots and saddlery, squatting in the front of their shops to catch the maximum light. Nearby are the rope makers, twirling the long, white strands of cotton (one of the main crops of the area), down the length of a bazaar passageway. Broken teapots and cups are mended in another corner, the fragments of porcelain drilled by a hand-bow before the metal staple is fixed. They will go back into service either in a private home or in one of the ubiquitous *chaikhanas,* or tea houses. Added colour is provided by shops selling *kolas,* the locally made highly-ornamented cap around which a turban is wound, each town having designs and shapes peculiar to itself.

There are also three of four shops that specialise in rugs and *kilims,* where with luck, one can find an unusual piece still in good condition, as well as old ikat *chapans* from as far north as Bokhara in Soviet Uzbekistan, and both old and new embroidery. (Prior to ikat weaving, the threads — usually silk — are tightly bound in such manner as to allow only the unbound part to be dyed. This process is repeated several times, resulting in each thread being multicoloured. Thus when arranged on the loom, a desired pattern can be woven.)

Many Uzbek mountain villagers come from remote areas into town in the spring, bringing some old and new pieces of domestic items either woven or embroidered, to sell in the Tashkurghan market, the most important before Mazar. (See Colour Plate 5.)

Facing the western approach to the old citadel is the small and compact carpet bazaar, which functions every day of the week except Fridays. Here also one can occasionally find an unusual and attractive piece, but at highly inflated prices. Both tourists and foreign residents of Kabul share the mistaken belief that prices must inevitably be lower here, near the source of production, that in the capital. This is not so. Older pieces are often sent to Mazar from Kabul simply to obtain a higher price.

Mazar-i-Sharif, the fourth largest city in Afghanistan, is the capital of Balkh Province, and an important commercial centre. In the large square dominating the town lies the most venerated shrine in Afghanistan. This is the alleged mausoleum of Hazrat Ali, the Prophet's son-in-law, rebuilt in the fifteenth century after its destruction by Genghis Khan two hundred years earlier. Both the actual mausoleum and the modern mosque adjacent to it are covered with painted faience tiles, mostly in turquoise blue and green with some gold. Hundreds of snow-white pigeons fly in constant circles around the domed halls of the shrine and come to rest in the gardens surrounding the mosque. The devout Sunni as well as the Shi'a Muslim believes there is a special merit in making a pilgrimage to this shrine during the forty days immediately following the Afghan *Nau Rouz,* or New Year, which falls on March 21st, the spring equinox.

From Mazar, there is a track going eastwards to Kunduz, capital of Kunduz Province, but this rough road, which crosses sparsely populated semi-desert, is not safe and is thus seldom used. Kunduz, which can be said to be the eastern limit of Afghan Turkestan, in common with the whole of Afghan Turkestan, is famous for its tradition of *buzkashi,* the spectacular national sport of the Turkomans.

Buzkashi, literally 'pulling the goat', requires superb horsemanship, tremendous stamina and strength, as well as great courage and the ability to endure considerable physical danger, strain and pain. The object of the game is for a horseman to try, against the opposition of anything up to a hundred or more riders, to carry a decapitated and disembowelled calf or goat and to drop it in front of the spectators. The powerful *buzkashi* horses are especially bred,

Seller of Uzbek kilims in Mazar-i-Sharif bazaar

Buzkashi

Buzkashi

trained and fed, and horse and rider work as one. There are few rules and no efforts are spared to force a rider to let go his goat. With a thick leather whip gripped between their teeth, and wearing a round fur hat bordered with Karaqul, a quilted coat open on their bare chests, leather trousers and boots with high heels, these rough, proud men evoke the age-old conquerors who ranged across the steppes of Central Asia. It is said that *buzkashi* was played in ancient times to keep the armies of Genghis Khan and others in fighting condition. (See Colour Plate 6).

From October to March, *buzkashi* is played regularly every weekend, much like rugger or soccer in Europe. In addition, a wealthy Turkoman may lay on a special *buzkashi* lasting two or three days to mark a major occasion, such as the birth of a first son, or a son's circumcision. Over one hundred horsemen may take part, with as many as one thousand guests travelling from outlying regions to attend this special event. They are fed and housed in the homes of relatives and friends of the host. Smaller *buzkashis,* involving only twenty-five or so players, are laid on for marriages, which customarily take place in the winter months when there are no agricultural activities.

Turning westward from Kunduz, itself the centre of a carpet producing district, one passes through the great traditional carpet weaving regions of Mazar, Aq Chah, Sheberghan, Andkhoy and Daulatabad. The paved section of the northern Circular Route ends at Sheberghan, and to continue the trip to Maimana, capital of Faryab Province and to all intents and purposes the western limit of Afghan Turkestan, the only public transport is the lumbering fifteen-hundred-kilo Russian lorry that 'does the line', that is, covers this rough part of the route leading to Herat. It is only four hundred and forty kilometres from Maimana to Herat, but the trip may take more than two days of exhausting yet exhilarating travel.

These much used lorries operate from a designated staging point, usually a tea house near the entrance of a town or village. Here the passenger is enticed or bullied by a *dallal* (broker) or the *kleenah*. As the name suggests, the *kleenah* keeps the vehicle clean, but is also the driver's apprentice. He stands just below the tailboard, clinging onto the lorry's superstructure, ever ready to jump down and place a wooden chock under a rear wheel should an incline prove too steep for the overladen lorry.

Passengers are seated on benches facing each other; the overflow squat on the floor filling every space available. As the lorry lurches over culverts, rocks and dried river beds, the passengers sway and pitch in rhythm, protecting their faces with the ends of their turbans or as best they can from the blast of fine dust that envelops them each time two lorries pass each other, and may Providence keep you from a following wind!

Another hazard of such a trip is the unforeseeable risk of the seasick traveller. Many a disaster has occurred in the packed interior of a lorry, with the poor victim unable to extricate himself in time. He is sometimes punished by being made to spend the rest of the trip standing on a foot-step at the outside of the truck, hanging on for dear life. The more fastidious drivers, before starting up, will demand of the prospective passengers: "Are there any *istefraqis* among you?" literally, 'any thrower uppers'. If a shamefaced man comes forward, he is made to sit at the very end of the lorry facing the open void.

For a slightly higher fare, two 'First-Class' passengers squeeze into a single seat next to the driver. All passengers arrive stiff, tired, dusty and thirsty. With their bundles of belongings, they disperse, some by foot, others taking the two-wheeled cart *(gaadi)* drawn by a hack whose harness is gaily decorated with bright red pompoms and garish coloured plastic flowers.

In all of the more remote provincial capitals, a focal point is the non-catering government hotel. Features they all share in common seem to be malodorous toilets with a non-functioning flushing system, and Afghan carpets on the floor of even the cheapest room. These old carpets of lovely mellowed browns and reds, enhanced by a beautiful clear indigo, are by now ruined through years of neglect and vandalism.

It is common to see a carpet with a piece cut out of it to accommodate a protruding section of wall, or a wood burning stove which is dismantled in the spring.

A more common alternative to the government hotel is the *chaikhana,* also called *samovar,* which in many places is Afghanistan's equivalent of the English country inn or the *auberge* of France. The tea house provides all the basic requirements needed by the weary traveller. Any qualms which he may have when a mountainous plateful of greasy *pillau* is plonked down in front of him are soon dispelled by the warm hospitality and spontaneous welcome. In fact, the foreigner may find two gristly lumps of rubbery meat buried in his rice instead of the customary solitary one.

A chaikhana or tea house in Mazar-i-Sharif where carpets are seen to be used

After a simple yet copious meal, either green or black tea is served, sometimes in small glass tumblers, but more often in handle-less porcelain bowls, reminiscent of the Chinese tea bowl. Each customer has his own small teapot and a saucer of boiled sweets or *nokles* (sugar coated almonds or chickpeas) through which he noisily sips.

The larger tea houses have a guest room which is shared by all those planning to stay the night. The tea house itself accommodates the overflow — a common event in a country where roads are seasonally cut by flash floods, rain storms or snow, and where mechanical breakdowns are ever common.

The owner of the tea house will always provide a *toshak* (a thin cotton-filled mattress), a blanket and sometimes even a pillow, which are placed on the floor ready for occupation. The sufficiently exhausted traveller soon falls asleep, and does not cavil at either the lack of hygiene or those little jumping or flying insects whose nocturnal activities become apparent only when he wakes to the raucous coughs of his fellow travellers just as dawn is breaking.

As a foreigner, one is always treated with particular kindness and consideration, and not without some curiosity. How is it that a respectable *khariji* (foreigner) is not riding in his own private car? After a few aloof sideward glances, the inevitable questions begin. Origin, family status and, not uncommonly, what one's salary is. In Afghan eyes, this is not impertinence, but rather a simple putting together of a jigsaw puzzle. It also provides him with material to enhance his own prestige when, later in the day, he will render an embellished account of the day's events to his friends or family. Here, sitting barefoot and cross-legged on a *kilim* or threadbare carpet, he will entertain the room at large with the smallest details of this new encounter.

As one approaches the wooded valley of Maimana, the rounded hills rise more steeply and compactly, their aspect changing dramatically with the seasons. In spring, the hillsides are tinged with green, the arid pastures flecked with a plant whose yellow flowers are used as a dye and is locally known as *isparak.* In midsummer, sparsely plated corn ripens in the heat-baked earth. For many winter months, a deep blanket of snow covers even the most travelled sections of this remote road, making it impassable for weeks at a time.

Nomads have always been a soul-stirring feature of the Afghan landscape, as their caravans follow the timeless migrations from the hot arid plains of Turkestan, into the cooler hills in search of fresh grazing. Many of these nomadic tribes still follow the traditional routes which lead into both Iran and Pakistan, and are responsible for much of the two-way smuggling which traditionally takes place across these borders.

Today some two million nomads, called *maldars* (strictly speaking, *maldar* refers to flock or herd owners, and *kuchi* is a pejorative word meaning 'gypsy'), or more popularly *kuchis,* still lead their caravans across the deserts

Part of a caravan

Children carried on a camel

and mountain passes of Afghanistan, following the seasons to seek warmth and pasture-land. A caravan may consist of only two or three families, with all their belongings loaded on a few donkeys and perhaps a single camel with one or two goats or sheep. Among the poorer groups both women and men walk alongside, and only the very young children, or a chicken tied by its leg to a tent pole, are perched on top of the mound of possessions on the donkey's back. A fierce, trained mastiff trots alongside to guard the family and its animals.

On the other hand, the caravan of a large, wealthy clan is a spectacular sight. Two score or more camels, each one covered with a carpet or heavy cloth, slowly walk in single file. Sitting high on the humps are the women of the tribe, with their babies or younger children. The women are heavily bedecked with gold or silver jewellery, long earrings, numerous bracelets and necklaces hung with pendants, and in each nostril a small silver stud. They are not veiled like the city women, but wear over their head a long black or red cloak which they pull across their face when passing foreign eyes. The camels are loaded with various woven bags, including *torbahs,* decorated with beads and small round mirrors which glitter in the sun. Chickens and new-born lambs, puppies or goats, as well as babies are packed in the side panniers and survey the world from atop this rocking nursery. Behind the camels a cloud of dust as far as the horizon envelops the thousand sheep and goats that follow up the rear.

Half a dozen large dogs, with ears clipped so as not to lose them in a fight, patrol the endless shifting mass of livestock, keeping a stray animal in line or stopping to bark a message to the shepherd should a sheep or goat fall sick or injured by the wayside.

Chapter 2

The Turkomans of Afghanistan

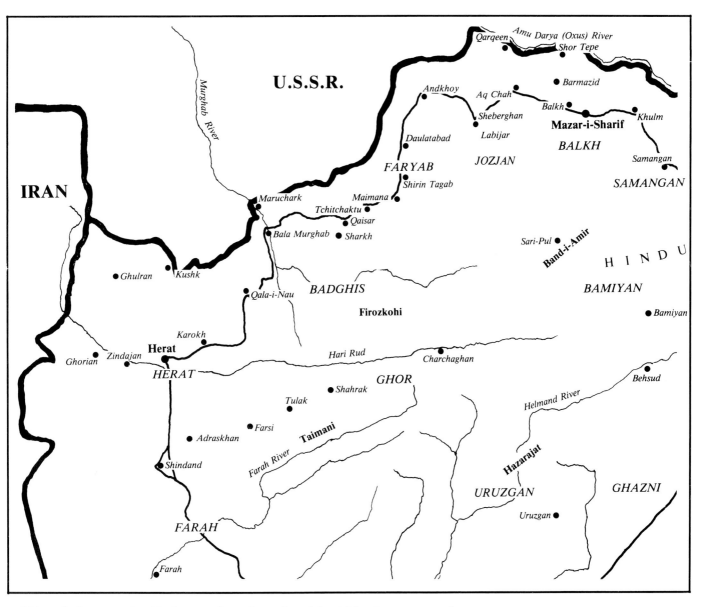

Although for centuries Turkomans have been found in Afghanistan, most of the four hundred thousand or so now living there came as refugees from the Soviet Union in the early 1920s and afterwards to escape from the initial Bolshevik suppression of Soviet Turkestan, and from the unpalatability of communism.

These Turkomans settled in what land was available, poor and arid though

Turkestan plain, the road to the Russian border

most of it was. Here they continued their traditional way of life, the men farming and rearing animals, the women employed in domestic activities and weaving carpets.

The Turkoman is a calm and dignified person, proud of and loyal to his lineage and antecedents. Of great courtesy and charm, he is extremely hospitable. Tolerant of strangers, honest and loyal in his business dealings, he is a devout Hanafi Sunni Muslim.

In common with men of the soil the world over — and especially those of nomadic traditions — the Turkoman is a traditionalist. Thus today, he and his womenfolk dress and eat, marry and bury, play and work much as did their forefathers. It is rare to see a Turkoman dressed in anything other than his traditional clothing which consists of a long cotton shirt over his baggy trousers, a waistcoat, long leather riding boots (or sandals) and a gaily striped *chapan* over his shoulders. On his head he will invariably wear a long turban of silk or fine cotton.

One notable difference, however, is that today — having become sedentary — the Turkoman generally lives in a mud-brick, flat-roofed compound. Nevertheless, even here, the traditional *yurt* is to be seen, often used as a day-room for the women and children, and sometimes used for housing the loom on which their carpets and rugs are woven.

The Turkoman is, physically, a tough character — as evinced by his love of *buzkashi*. Understandably he respects those whom he believes to have the qualities which he admires. The following anecdote illustrates the point.

In his early days in Afghanistan, the author — who is no horseman — admired a large white stallion belonging to a Turkoman with whom he was doing business. The author was invited to mount. Fearing a broken limb less than the Turkoman's contempt, he did so. At first the stallion merely ambled, but encouraged by his rider started trotting, then cantered and quickly broke into a gallop. Approaching a narrow bridge from the opposite side, there appeared a well-laden *gaadi* drawn by a trotting hack. It soon became evident that the noble and proud stallion considered that he should have right of way, for he increased his gallop. His more cautious rider decided otherwise and, in trying to pull up his enthusiastic and headstrong mount, discovered what insensitive mouths Turkoman horses had. Neither stallion nor hack showed the slightest concern as each approached his own entrance to the bridge. Visions of a head-on collision, or an impossible leap over the oncoming menace. . . using all his strength the rider just managed to pull up his horse in time, and trembling with fear and shock, saw the *gaadi* trot unconcernedly on its way. The author, wet and sweaty turned back towards the *serai* where he was greeted with the laconic comment, "That was a short ride".

Probably because the Turkoman was aware of what had happened, the author passed muster, for he was not only invited to spend the night at the Turkoman's home, but also urged to take part in a *buzkashi* the next day!

The Turkoman's domestic life is a well-ordered one. From an early age the children, who never suffer from lack of parental love or care, are trained in the tribal traditions, and soon learn their responsibilities within the family group.

From an early age boys will begin to spend an ever-increasing amount of time with the menfolk — particularly in the evenings and at meals, when they will be taught how to eat correctly from the communal dishes, and using only their right hand. Among Muslims the world over, the left hand is considered the 'dirty' hand and is used in cleaning oneself. Thus it is considered very rude to offer or give anything with the left hand, and one eats using only the right. Hence it will be realised that the severance of a thief's right hand has far deeper connotations than merely losing a limb. As they grow older, the boys learn to wait on their elders and on guests, and whilst always partaking fully in these events, they will generally be silent, for it is considered unseemly for

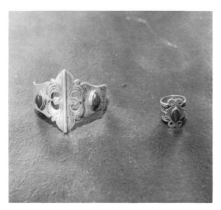

Turkoman bracelet and ring

those with no experience of life to do other than assimilate wisdom and knowledge from their elders.

At a very early age, the girls are taught to mind those who are even younger than they are. Thus it is not unusual to see a three-year-old cleaning or comforting an infant. Apart from taking a progressively important part in the various domestic activities of the compound, girls will soon squat alongside their mother or aunt, sister-in-law or grandmother, and be taught the art of carpet making.

On reaching the age of puberty, girls will wear the veil, for modesty precludes any but the closest male relatives from seeing the face of any girl of marriageable age or, indeed, any married women. Red is a popular colour amongst the Turkoman women for their veils, as is yellow. Unmarried girls can be distinguished by the flatter *kola* or round embroidered cap worn under the veil.

Turkoman wedding procession

When visiting a Turkoman compound for whatever reason, one is always accompanied by a male who will go ahead, knock loudly on the wooden door, warning the womenfolk of a stranger's advent. By the time that one is led inside, all the women will have disappeared from sight. However, it does happen that when examining a carpet still on the loom, one becomes aware of curious eyes peeping from behind a curtain. Good manners dictate that such mutual curiosity should be ignored.

The modesty of their womenfolk is jealously guarded by the Turkoman. I was once asked by a Turkoman friend to get him a polaroid camera — even though he was the proud owner of an ordinary one. Juma Morad had fled the Soviet Union when he was about eleven years old, crossing the Amu Darya River with the help of some nomads. He had no family whatsoever in Afghanistan, but in time married and had three children (today he has four). He was inordinately fond and proud of his family, and wished to send a photograph of them to his relatives whom he had recently contacted in the USSR. On being asked why he wanted a polaroid, he replied that it was unthinkable to allow a stranger to develop a film of his wife!

On reaching the age of sixteen or so, a boy will get married, the match having been arranged by his parents — sometimes, even before his birth! Marriage in a Turkoman family does not mean leaving home.

The groom, together with his young wife will live in his parental compound, and if at school, will continue with his studies. Otherwise, both will continue to play their respective roles, gradually assuming increased responsibilities, and all the time strengthening the family unit.

Of the Turkomans in Afghanistan, by far the greater majority are the Ersaris. This tribe is made up of four main clans and approximately fifty sub-clans. The chart (see page 28) shows the structure of the Ersari tribe as held in the memory of several of its elders. By no means claiming to be complete, or even entirely accurate, it nevertheless shows the complexity of the tribal lineage and ancestry, perhaps making the identification of Ersari carpets a bit clearer and more meaningful.

By and large, the Ersari carpets are not so fine as those of some other Turkoman weavers, especially the Tekkes and Saruqs. Nonetheless, they continue to make attractive and durable pieces, always double wefted and with a strong individual character, generally portraying the *fil-pai* (elephant foot) motif in one of its several forms, or the Bokhara pattern. A continuous change is taking place in design composition. This is due to several reasons, not least of which is fashion and the dictates of commercial interests. Another reason is the increasing tendency of the Ersaris to intermarry not only with Turkomans of other clans within the tribe who bring with them some of their own individual clan motifs, but also with members of other tribes, notably the Uzbek. Here it should be stated that the name 'Uzbek' has come to mean a

Turkoman women

generic term for all the various clans and tribes who lived in the relatively newly defined state of Uzbekistan. In spite of the variance amongst the Uzbek, they are all Turkic, but some are very much more akin in looks and customs to the Turkoman. In Afghanistan, many of these live in the Andkhoy area, and it is primarily with these Uzbek people that the Turkoman would intermarry.

The Ersari Tribal Structure as Recounted by Elders

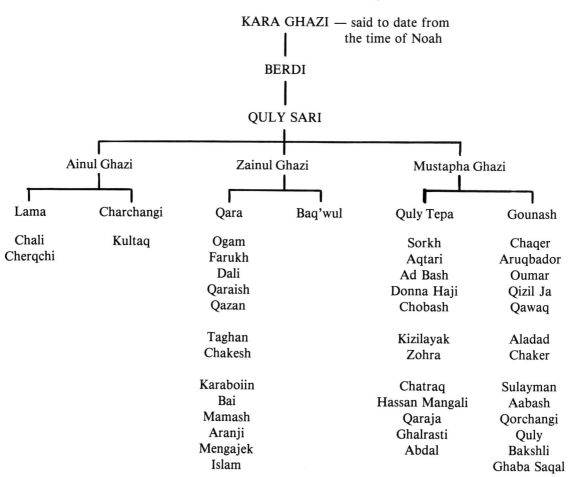

KARA GHAZI — said to date from the time of Noah

BERDI

QULY SARI

Ainul Ghazi		Zainul Ghazi		Mustapha Ghazi	
Lama	Charchangi	Qara	Baq'wul	Quly Tepa	Gounash
Chali	Kultaq	Ogam		Sorkh	Chaqer
Cherqchi		Farukh		Aqtari	Aruqbador
		Dali		Ad Bash	Oumar
		Qaraish		Donna Haji	Qizil Ja
		Qazan		Chobash	Qawaq
		Taghan		Kizilayak	Aladad
		Chakesh		Zohra	Chaker
		Karaboiin		Chatraq	Sulayman
		Bai		Hassan Mangali	Aabash
		Mamash		Qaraja	Qorchangi
		Aranji		Ghalrasti	Quly
		Mengajek		Abdal	Bakshli
		Islam			Ghaba Saqal

The Tekke Turkomans of Afghanistan

The Tekkes, one of the renowned Turkoman tribes, arrived in Afghanistan about fifty years ago. An elderly Tekke recounted to me their emigration from Soviet Turkmenistan into Afghanistan in 1931, when five hundred families from Bairmali near Merv left their homes to escape the Bolshevik supression of that area. He remembers vividly the long, hazardous journey by camel caravan through the desert. They crossed the Amu Darya River in the region of Maimana and moved westward. Some members of the caravan stopped at Sharkh and the rest continued to Herat. He remembers that here they were stopped by two policemen who asked for protection money and when the

Tekkes refused, some of their elders were put into prison. The governor heard of this mistreatment some days later and had the policemen publicly nailed by their ears to a wooden post. The Tekkes were offered land further south in Farah but they could not successfully cultivate this barren and arid soil and so, two years later, they returned to Herat. Some settled here, some in Ghorian, seventy kilometres west of Herat, and the remaining families wended their way eastward to Mazar. They were given land near Balkh by the governor who had known some of the elders when he was ambassador in Ashkhabad, the capital of Soviet Turkmenistan. Today the village of Barmazid, a few kilometres north-east of Balkh, is the home of about two hundred Tekke families.

These tribal people brought few possessions with them, and much of what dowry jewellery they had was sold in their efforts to make a new life for themselves. They did bring with them, however, their culture, traditions, and their age-old weaving skills, which were immediately put into practice wherever they settled in their new land of adoption.

Thus we see that in Afghanistan, these Tekkes from Merv settled in four distinct areas — Herat, Ghorian, Sharkh and Barmazid.

The Tekkes of Afghanistan, who are fiercely proud of their antecedents, do not give their daughters in marriage to anyone not of their tribe. In Sharkh, the story is still told about a stranger who eloped with a Tekke girl. He was soon caught, castrated, and put to death. A short-lived romance! The Tekkes of Sharkh take it as their right to be the first to offer hospitality to a stranger, especially if he is in the carpet trade, and it is they who assume responsibility for his well-being and safety.

The Saruq (often 'Saryk') Turkomans of Afghanistan

The Saruqs are a Turkoman tribe, settled in Maruchark, a group of three villages on the Afghanistan-USSR frontier in the northern corner of Badghis Province, north of Balah Murghab.

They number only some fifteen hundred houses in Afghanistan, though in Soviet Turkmenistan they are to be found all the way up the Murghab River as far as Merv. Apart from the settlement at Maruchark, there is another small group of Saruqs in Herat. Here some twenty or so families weave both their own traditional design as well as the Mauri design — that is, the Tekke *gul*.

This is what may give rise to the common confusion between the place name Maruchark and Mauri Sharkh.

Mauri Sharkh is a meaningless term, erroneously used — especially in Germany — to describe the quality/origin of a Tekke carpet from Sharkh. (Sharkh is one of the four places in Afghanistan where Tekke Turkomans are settled, but Mauri refers to a quality of carpet made in and around Herat, where it is marketed.) The Saruqs claim kinship with the Salors who are found on the north side of the Murghab River. There are no Salors in Afghanistan.

For the sake of convenience, the Saruq carpet is listed under the Herat production, where it is marketed.

The Yamoud Turkomans of Afghanistan

Yamouds in Afghanistan are few, and are only to be found in Herat, where they occupy about one hundred houses in the west of the city.

In the early 1920s, some three hundred families of the Junad clan of Yamouds from the region of Merv in Soviet Turkmenistan, sought refuge in Afghanistan. They were given land by the Afghan Emir, Amanullah Khan, but hardly had they begun to establish themselves than two-thirds of their people

A Turkoman village

died, probably from some epidemic. The remaining Yamouds are now integrated into urban life, yet still maintain their customs and tribal purity by not intermarrying.

The Qarqeen Turkomans of Afghanistan

The Quarqeen, albeit Turkomans, are not Ersaris — though after living in this extreme northern region of Afghanistan for one hundred and fifty years or more, they now think of themselves as members of the Ersari family. The majority live in Qarqeen, situated on the Amu Darya River north-west of Mazar. This district is made up of three villages in which live some ten thousand Qarqeen Turkomans. To a large degree, it is a poor community which has remained unaffected by modern change. About seventy per cent of the people still live in *yurts,* in a barren and remote land where they lead a purely agricultural life. Their *yurt* doors made from wood of the willow are fashioned by the Qaraja clan of Ersaris, traditionally known as the craftsmen who specialise in working this wood. Other Qarqeens are found in small communities, mostly scattered in the Aq Chah and Kunduz areas.

One main difference between the Qarqeen and the Ersari, is the more sophisticated manner in which the former control water distribution in irrigation.

The Saltuq Turkomans of Afghanistan

The Saltuqs are a people who claim to be descendants of the Turkic Saljuk dynasty which ruled in Afghanistan during the twelfth century. In any case, they have been settled in Afghan Turkestan for centuries. They number some three thousand souls and are concentrated in five villages, three of which are in the Labijar district in the Sheberghan area, and two near Aq Chah.

The Saltuqs consider themselves to be of aristocratic descent. Indeed, they never marry outside their tribe and they are regarded in the same way by the Ersaris who, though referring to them as princely, at the same time do not consider them to be of pure Ersari Turkoman origin.

Chapter 3

The Making of Afghan Carpets

The Sheep

Of the eight or so classified breeds of sheep in Afghanistan only five contribute their wool to the country's carpet industry. The principal breeds that are used in making Afghan carpets are the Karaqul from the north and the Ghilzai found predominantly in the south, as well as the Kandahari, the Hazaragi, the Beluchi from Nimroz Province and the strains found around Herat which include the Arabi and Herati sheep. All are of the fat-tailed variety but because of cross-breeding and migratory movement, as well as no altogether precise geographic boundaries, it is difficult to be absolutely categoric when referring to any specific breed of sheep.

By far the most commonly used wool comes from the Karaqul sheep, indigenous to Uzbekistan in the south-west Soviet Union, as well as northern Afghanistan. The Karaqul sheep has a dual fleece, which means two types of wool growing simultaneously. The outer fleece has longer staples than the soft crinkly wool of the inner fleece; both are hardwearing and lustrous and when carefully sorted and blended provide ideal wool for Afghan carpets.

The Karaqul sheep, generally grey or black in colour and recognisable by the kink in its tail lying over the heart-shaped lobes, is a hardy animal, living in regions with extremes of temperature ranging from $-30°C$ up to $48°C$ in the shade. It is also renowned in the fur trade for the tightly-curled glossy newborn lambskins called variously Karaqul, Broadtail, Astrakhan and Persian lamb, sold annually at international fur auctions in London and Leningrad. Some six million Karaqul sheep are raised on the northern slopes of Afghanistan alone.

The Ghilzai, or nomad sheep, is variously coloured. Its fat tail gets very large and its wool tends to be coarse. Much of this wool is bought by the Hazaras from the nomads who in summer graze their flocks high up in the Hindu Kush and around Behsud in the mountains of the Hazarajat. It is used in commercial Hazara *kilims* as well as for warp yarn which is sold to Turkomans who use it in the production of cheaper quality carpets.

The Kandahari breed comes from the semi-desert regions around Kandahar, yet can be found as far north as Herat. Also a fat-tailed species, it is smaller than the Karaqul, all white with black patches on its face and sometimes on its body. Often it has black feet and one or two black ears. The finest of its white wool is exported to the USSR; some of the coarser and harder-wearing wool is bought by Turkomans who use it mainly for the white motifs in their designs.

The Hazaragi breed, native to the central mountains of the Hazarajat, are variously black, dark brown, reddy-brown, fawn and off-white. The wool is very soft and fine, and is suitable for weaving into cloth. It is also used by the Hazaragi people for weaving domestic *kilims*.

The Beluchi sheep is another fat-tailed variety, usually white though with legs and head black or brown. It has longer ears than most breeds in the south and its wool is fine.

The various breeds and strains of sheep around Herat, including the Arabi, Herati and Gaadic, furnish wool used for Beluch and Beluch-type carpets. The

South of Balkh

Dipping sheep

various steps involved in preparing yarn for dyeing and final weaving are generally the same for the different types of wool.

The Wool

Shearing, which is done by hand, takes place in the spring, starting about mid-April, and again in the autumn during September, when it may be only partial depending on the condition of the sheep. The spring clip, with a seven-month growth, provides the better wool and is invariably used in the finer quality of carpet. Wool from the autumn shearing was not, traditionally, used for carpet making. However, with the commercialisation of the Afghan Turkoman carpet the autumn clip is now increasingly made into carpet yarn.

Turkomans claim that in former times, when carpet weaving was primarily for domestic use and the sorting of wool was done with a care that present-day commercialisation does not allow, their carpets never cockled if wetted. Even today, many weavers are loath to mix spring wool with wool from the autumn clip. Cockling in Afghan woven goods is due to bad mixing of wool from different parts of the fleece and where hair or *kemp* is mixed, the degree of lustre is further diminished.

After shearing, the fleeces are twisted and rolled up on themselves in the same manner as done in Europe. As shearing may take place out in the open grazing regions far from any habitation, the fleeces are transported to the local bazaar either by small lorry or by camel caravans.

The lanolin content of Afghan wool is so low that scouring takes place very rarely and only when judged necessary. Often the dipping of sheep prior to shearing is considered sufficient. This usually means passing the sheep through a muddy stream! In any case, the constant dust storms would put the cleaning of wool on a par with that of the Augean stables.

The fleeces are next sorted by colour, and the wool graded by quality; the coarse, rough hairs, known as *kemp,* and the dags, or dirt clotted wool, being put aside. In Afghanistan some hand carding is still done by the older men and women. The most common method is to place a block of wood embedded with metal spikes on the ground, and to pull the wool through the spikes repeatedly until all the fibres lie in the same direction and the longer fibres are separated from the shorter ones. Up to one kilo of wool a day can be carded by this method. 'Butter-pat' carders are not used in Afghanistan.

Until recently most wool used in Turkoman carpets was put through a locally-made belt-driven machine similar to an 'opening' machine used in woollen mills abroad. The result was effective but gave rise to the temptation — often irresistible — to mix in 'dead' wool (also called plucked wool) that is, wool from dead sheep. In Aq Chah, for example, there is a factory processing skins for tanning, the wool of which is removed in lime pits. This dead wool, sold locally and cheaply as a by-product, is dry, brittle and lacks all lustre.

In 1977, the Afghanistan government banned the use of these machines, but after vehement protests rescinded its order. In 1978 the new government again imposed the ban. These periods of restriction encouraged the importation of machine-spun yarn from Pakistan, some of which is very cheap and of poor quality, being dry and dull wool of short staple resulting in much fibre shedding. Here we see the unfortunate and gradual introduction of machine-spun yarn in Afghan goods. This trend will no doubt accelerate when the government-owned wool mill at Kandahar goes into operation. This will be another departure from tradition; until now it could be said that all the yarn used in the Afghan carpet production was entirely hand spun and hand treated at every stage.

Nevertheless, most of the yarn in the Afghan carpet industry is still hand

Sorting wool

spun. This is generally done by both men and women, often Arabis who are principally spinners and not weavers. In the Aq Chah region, for example, the village of Laila specialises in spinning yarn for the pile, and the village of Keltasharkh in yarn for warp and weft.

Not surprisingly, wool that has been well sorted and carded can be more easily and finely spun than ill-sorted wool. The regularity and constancy of the yarn is important for both a clean and even back and because any irregularity in the thickness of yarn used for either warp or weft will create tensions which often lead to cockling. Prior to dyeing, the balls of wool are made into skeins.

Sorting wool

Dyeing

Chemical dyestuffs of different manufacture and of varying quality are used in the dyeing of wool for Afghan carpets and rugs. Black, often used in the cheaper Afghan goods, frequently oxidises into an anthracite grey. Now that the world shortage of indigo (used to meet the universal demand for blue jeans) has eased, one may hope that less black will be used in the Afghan production. Some blue dyes, other than indigo, are also becoming increasingly common. They are cheaper and easier to use than indigo and give a bright royal blue which all too often oxidises into a muddy grey after a relatively short time. (See Colour Plate 83). In the early 1970s, cheap dyes smuggled from Pakistan and Iran were found in most bazaars of the carpet-producing areas, especially in Herat. Fortunately, the use of these smuggled chemical dyestuffs is now diminishing, though many a well-made piece — especially of the Beluch-type — is still being ruined by gaudy metallic greens, purples and pinks.

However, the trend in several centres of production, namely Andkhoy, Kunduz and Herat, to revert to the use of natural dyes is undeniable, even though the preparation of these, from the gathering of the raw materials to the final brewing, is both more laborious and time-consuming than simply opening up a tin. This naturally is reflected in the price of the finished piece.

Madder (local name *royan*) is one of the principal natural dyestuffs used in Afghanistan, whose warm, mellow reds are so loved by Turkoman weavers. It is used either alone or in combination with other dyes, to produce shades varying from rose-pinks to red-browns. The roots of this spindly bush are dug up from late autumn to early spring, snow and frost permitting, when the sap is at its lowest. There is little danger of killing the plant because the bush regenerates from only a small segment of the root left in the ground. Madder grows extensively in the region of Herat and the northern districts of Balkh and Shor Tepe; to a lesser degree around Sheberghan, Andkhoy and Shirin Tagab.

The root is cut into small pieces about one centimetre in length and allowed to dry for up to forty days, after which the pieces are broken down with a pestle and finally ground into a coarse powder. The bark of the root gives a pink-rose dye, while the inner core, depending on its thickness, gives a reddish brown. The thickness of the root determines the shade of red; thus, a section of root the diameter of, say, a cigarette, renders a bright pinky red, and a section of the diameter of a man's thumb renders a rich mahogany brown. Madder, although plentiful, is nevertheless a costly material because of the quantity required and the laborious process of preparation.

It is virtually impossible for wool to 'take' natural dyestuffs without a mordant. Madder is no exception, and in this case alum locally called *zantch* and barley sour dough are used. The complex process for dyeing a *seer* (seven kilos) of wool is roughly as follows: three hundred grams of powder alum are dissolved in sufficient boiling water to cover the yarn. When this has cooled to

Dyeing wool

about 60°C, five hundred grams of barley sour dough are stirred into the brew. The yarn is immersed and allowed to soak until it begins to ferment and gives off a strong smell. This can take from five to ten days, depending on the temperature. (In winter the vat is heated to keep it from freezing.) The wool is then taken out and dried.

The next stage is to boil large pieces of a special type of wood whose sap has properties that fix the dyes. The wood is removed and in this water, one *seer* of powdered madder is placed, together with the yarn, and brought to the boil. At this point, the brushwood fire is extinguished and the yarn is left to soak for some five hours. It is then taken out, wrung dry and any fragments of madder shaken out, and rinsed in water in which has been boiled peganum harmala *(ashqar)* which gives it a sheen; it is rinsed again in clear water and then sun dried.

Sparak is the Uzbek name used in Afghan Turkestan for a wild flower which grows on the steppes and is particularly abundant around Maimana. It is also known as *zahr-i-choub,* 'yellow wood'. From afar, *sparak* resembles ragwort *(Senecio Jacobea)* and, like ragwort, it is also poisonous to cattle. The florettes of this plant are collected in April and May and left to dry, then ground into powder. The mordants and general dyeing process are the same as described above, except that less *sparak* dye is required and the yarn must steep for five to ten days longer in the mordant.

To obtain green, the yarn is first dyed with *sparak* and then with indigo. Walnut peel, pomegranate peel and wheat straw are other sources of natural dyes. Walnut peel, the section around the shell, gives a dark brown and is often combined with madder to darken the reds. Pomegranate peel and wheat straw give different tones of medium to light brown.

The mordant for each of the above is also alum, but the dyeing process is somewhat simpler: water, in which three hundred grams of alum have been boiled, is heated to 90°C. The dyestuff is added and the brew is brought again to the boil. When it has cooled back to 90°C, the yarn is introduced and allowed to soak for three to four hours.

Kermes (from the Arabic *qirmiz,* whence our crimson), the dried bodies of insects found in oak bark, was a common dye in the past. The cost and extremely limited supply in Afghanistan, however, make it unlikely that it will again be used to any extent.

The indigo dye used today in Afghanistan is entirely factory made, but it is, by chemical analysis, virtually indistinguishable from the dye obtained from the plant itself. The traditional method among many Ersari Turkomans for dyeing with indigo was as follows: marrow from sheep or beef bones was put in a vat with a lump of wheat sour dough. Indigo was stirred into this and the vat left out in the sun. The yarn was dipped in water in which a handful of barley meal had been mixed, wrung dry and then placed in the vat of indigo to steep for fifteen days. The vat was covered to reduce loss by evaporation, and left to ferment in the natural heat of the sun. If the results were not to the dyer's satisfaction, more bone marrow and sour dough were added and the yarn steeped for a further period of up to five days. This method, however, is no longer used.

Although indigo dyeing by fermentation is still carried out today by the old dyemasters who are reluctant to adopt the newer, quicker methods, the two most common present-day processes are as follows:
1. Crushed peganum harmala *(ashqar)* is boiled in water and, when cool, the indigo is added. The yarn is left to steep in this brew, which is kept at a steady lukewarm heat for two to twelve hours, depending on the outside temperature. In winter a brushwood fire is lit under the vat and in summer packed snow from the distant mountains is sometimes used to keep the temperature down. The wool is then removed from the vat, wrung dry, sun dried and redipped.

Drying wool

This process is repeated two or three times.

2. Crushed peganum harmala is boiled in water. When this has cooled to 60°C, equal weights of indigo and a hyperchlorite bleach (*safidi qandi,* used to bleach sugar) which, when mixed with water produces chlorine, are stirred into the brew. The yarn is steeped in this for twenty minutes, removed and sun dried, and then washed again in the water in which yarn has been dyed red. This emphasises the blue.

There is a simple test to verify if the blue in a relatively new carpet, which has not been subjected to chemical washing, is indeed genuine indigo as opposed to 'instant blue'. A small amount of spittle or hot water is rubbed into the pile which then, if indigo, should give off an unmistakable smell of ammonia.

Wool which appears black on the fleece is, in fact, dark brown and when spun into yarn, this is quite obvious. However, this wool dyed with indigo may appear black, especially in the pile of a new carpet. The indigo tone is more apparent on the back of a carpet than in the pile itself.

In all dyeing processes, the dyer's own individual technique will have a bearing on the end results, but equally important is the original shade of the yarn being dyed. Thus, a white wool will have a much brighter colour than a grey wool, both having been subjected to exactly the same red dyestuffs. After dyeing, the wool is basically of the same colour but varying in tone, which is the reason for the incredibly harmonious range of reds and subtle blending of colours in Afghan carpets. The reds never clash!

Undyed, untreated brown and white wool and natural camel hair are also used in the production of Afghan carpets.

In older Afghan pieces sometimes whole areas of one colour, say the red or the indigo, have worn at a different rate from the other colours, resulting in areas of high and low pile. This is due to bad dyeing techniques and frequently to the use of iron in the mistaken belief that it will increase the strength of the mordant. It is an old wives' tale that a handful of nails thrown into the vat will make for purer and faster colouring (this is not to be confused with the proper use of iron mordanting). Too much iron renders the wool hard, with the result that it becomes brittle and the areas so dyed will show early signs of wear.

The Loom

Afghan weavers always use a horizontal loom. This is the most basic type of loom and is traditionally and exclusively used by nomadic tribes as it can easily be dismantled and transported. The loom consists of two wooden end beams placed on two side beams to which they are bolted, thus forming a rectangular frame. The end beams are firmly anchored to four stumps hammered into the ground and tightened by a tourniquet lashing or a screw bolt. The frame of the loom is usually of poplar, a cheap and fast growing wood, which is used extensively for building and furniture making.

A partly finished purdah on a horizontal loom

The warp threads are stretched lengthwise between the end beams in a figure eight, and are often dampened to increase tensions. To prevent slipping, mud or a flour paste is packed on the warp threads around the two end beams to fix them securely. Weaving only begins when this paste has caked hard.

A few ateliers with vertical looms have now been established in Kabul. The weavers are young boys seated on a bench facing their work. This is not a traditional method of Afghan carpet weaving. A goodly proportion of these rugs are of fine quality, often copies of Persian designs in silk or part silk. One cannot help wondering whether in time Kabul, with no carpet making tradition, will become a centre of production.

The vast majority of Turkoman weavers are women and girls, though

Weaving kilims

among the Turkomans, and especially among the Uzbeks, there is an increasing number of boys and youths who are learning this craft. They are usually unmarried, since the responsibilities of marriage force them to abandon this means of livelihood. The Beluch and Beluch-type goods are always woven by women or girls.

When beginning a carpet, the weaver (or weavers) squats on a plank placed immediately under the surface of warp threads at one end of the loom. As the work progresses, the weaver moves forward sitting now on the pile itself supported by the plank which is also moved forward. The only instruments used are the heavy metal 'comb' for beating down the wefts and a knife for cutting the pile yarn after the knot has been tied. Sometimes this knife ends in a small hook which is used to raise the lower warp thread, but usually this is done by hand, as is the actual tying of the knot. A pair of hand shears similar to those used for shearing sheep is used for clipping the pile at the end of the day.

Turkish or Ghiordes knot (symmetric)

Weaving

Turkoman carpet designs are woven entirely from memory and graph-paper patterns are used only when resuscitating old designs, or weaving totally new and non-traditional, therefore unfamiliar, designs.

A common fault in oriental carpets is a too close clipping of the pile in order to delineate the design more clearly. When this occurs, ridges formed by the barely covered warp become apparent and, of course, the life of the carpet is much reduced. Naturally, in countries where it is the custom to remove one's shoes on entering a room, the wear is a slower process.

The width of the carpet being woven determines the number of weavers needed. Weavers only move forward; the width of their working front will be as far as they can comfortably reach either side, generally about seventy-five centimetres.

An apprentice is placed next to an experienced adult weaver who not only supervises his work, but also ensures that the wefts are beaten down to an even tension to avoid a distortion in the design.

The Persian or Senneh knot is used in all Afghan carpets. Only very rarely — if at all these days — will one see a Turkish or Ghiordes knot. The difference between these two knots, about which much has been written, is illustrated here.

A carpet starts and ends in a band of flat weave called the *kilim*. In some regions, this *kilim* displays a design; in others, it is made up of lateral bands of colour; sometimes it is embroidered, sometimes plain, dyed or undyed. The variety and ingenuity of these end finishings are in themselves fascinating.

Many Turkomans are very poor and it is only the wealthier ones who can afford to have in their compounds a room devoted entirely to the housing of a loom, and big enough to hold a loom on which a large, say, 300cm x 400cm carpet can be made. This is why most large carpets are woven during the summer months, when the loom can be assembled for use outside. In winter, the production of rugs is markedly higher. In this book the term 'rug' is used for sizes up to but not including 8ft. x 5ft. (240cm x 150cm) and the term 'carpet' for sizes of 8ft. x 5ft. and larger.

A superstition common to most Turkomans in Afghanistan is putting a match to the fringe of a newly-woven piece and burning a small amount of wool. A wish is made that the carpet will be sold as quickly as the burned wool flares up.

Persian or Senneh knot (asymmetric)

Chapter 4

The Nomad Dwelling and Its Furnishings

Although Turkomans in Afghanistan are now a sedentary people, they were originally nomads, herding their flocks of sheep and goats across the rolling steppes of Central Asia. They lived in *yurts,* those circular domed tents seen from Outer Mongolia to the Caspian Sea. These wood framed tents, easily dismantled and reassembled, were lined and roofed with felt and skirted with thick reed matting, the whole being bound with woven tent bands. During winter, an open fire burned in the centre of the *yurt,* the smoke slowly leaving through a chimney hole in the roof. Fuel was dried manure, which gave off a pungent smell and soon blackened the felt walls and ceiling. Traditionally, a *yurt* constructed for a newly wed couple was white.

Building a yurt

The inside closure of the *yurt* was a carpet of special design called a *purdah* (curtain). Along the banks of the Amu Darya (Oxus) River and in a few inland settlements, there are still some Turkomans who live permanently in *yurts,* but these are now closed by a wooden door and no longer have a *purdah.*

Not surprisingly, in this largely self-sufficient and ovine-based economy wool was, and is, used extensively. Besides carpets and rugs, the Turkomans produced countless items made with wool for their daily domestic needs and *yurt* furnishings, wood and metal being extremely difficult to come by and, not being flexible, not so easy to transport. Having no furniture, they stored their clothes and household possessions in woven and knotted bags of different shapes and sizes, often of magnificent workmanship and design, each of which had a specific purpose. These bags were hung on the inside of the *yurt,* or placed on the ground and used as cushions.

Yurt

In every family, a minimum of tent bags was necessary for the storing of their possessions. Thus, the wealth and status of the family had a decided bearing on the number of bags owned. Wealth implied a greater number of possessions, while status determined the number of bags which a girl would bring in her dowry.

When a girl approached marriageable age — usually in her early teens — she and the other women in her family would start to weave carpets, bags and other pieces for her dowry. If a would-be suitor was not considered acceptable, the girl's father would answer that the dowry pieces were not yet completed. This tactful answer saved any loss of face. On the other hand, if the match was considered suitable, a tacit agreement was reached and the weaving of the pieces was accelerated!

Amongst the Turkomans of Afghanistan, there appears no hard and fast rule as to what woven pieces or jewellery constitute a dowry. Much depends on the standing of the parties involved. However, the number must be adequate, that much is certain, otherwise loss of face ensues for all concerned.

There is no set rule concerning what pieces make up a dowry, providing that it meets a minimum requirement. The following list was made by the head of a respected family of the Farukh clan from near Aq Chah, and comprises the dowry of both his mother and first wife, sixty and thirty years ago:

Black goats' hair tents

7a

Colour Plate 7a *A striking example of a finely woven old TAGHAN JUWAL. One of a pair and now backless, this dowry piece is noteworthy for having pale green silk in the secondary guls and for the inclusion of* kermes *(cochineal) in the centre of the primary gul. The light indigo of duck-egg blue colour of the double ram horn motif in the border suggests that this juwal was woven in Taghan-Labijar. (See page 93). (Circa 1920; 152 x 97cm)*

Shir Khosrow Paiwand

7/8

Colour Plate 7 A semi-antique JUWAL. The design is the alma gul *or apple blossom, associated with the Beshirs, of which the typical dark blue border guard is a good example. This one measures 137 x 84cm and is somewhat larger than the average.*

Colour Plate 8 An example of a very fine semi-antique JALLAR PAIDAR, size 140 x 25cm, the two ends are 70cm long.
Courtesy Pieter van Aalst, Breda, Holland, private collection

9

10

Colour Plate 9 A JALLAR, knotted and piled, woven in Andkhoy depicting the traditional Turkoman design from which the Zaher Shahi design — so called because King Zaher liked it and encouraged its use — was developed. This piece is woven in seven colours: dark indigo, royal blue, dark cherry red, red, orange, white and a greenish blue. (118 x 41cm).
Author's collection

Colour Plate 10 JALLAR. Flat woven with bastani *design.*
Courtesy Pieter van Aalst, Breda, Holland, private collection

1 *purdah*
1 *jallar paidar*
13 *jallars/torbahs,* both knotted and piled and flat woven
2 pair of *juwals*
2 salt bags
2 pairs *kola-i-chergh*
1 6m² carpet
1 *namad*
2 1.5m² rugs
3 tent bands

juwal gul

Among the traditional *yurt* furnishings are:

The Juwal or Choval

The largest *yurt* bag (always made in pairs) was the *juwal.* When migrating, these were hung one on either side of a camel, thus giving rise to the term 'camel bag'. Today, however, only seldom is a *juwal* actually used in this way, and then always in connection with wedding processions. Firmly implanted in the author's memory is a most picturesque scene, that of a heavily veiled bride with all her vivid adornments, sitting on a platform perched on a camel dressed 'overall'. In one *juwal* were three young bridesmaids, while in the other was another bridesmaid and a matron of honour, all in their best clothes and sumptuously bedecked with silver jewellery.

Juwals are still made in Afghanistan but none can compare with those old Tekke pieces of superb workmanship and exquisite design smuggled in from the USSR, often containing motifs in silk, and which are sold for outrageous prices in some Kabul carpet shops.

Current production of *juwals* comes from all the main weaving centres throughout Afghan Turkestan, particularly around Mazar, and are destined either for dowry pieces or merely for the commercial market. The design most frequently reproduced is known in Afghanistan as the *juwal gul* (see drawing) and is attributed, rightly or wrongly, to the clan of Chobash, mainly located in the Sheberghan and Mazar areas. The next most widely executed design is the *alma gul* of the Beshirs, made in the Kunduz region. (See Colour Plate 7).

In the Herat area, the Tekkes and Yamouds made *juwals* in a flat weave, though unlike the older pieces where sometimes a design band is knotted and piled, these are now entirely flat woven. Natural dyestuffs are nearly always used in this type.

Around Mazar, one can still find flat-woven and piled *juwals* made by Ersaris, probably Dalis, with various embroidered bands. However, production of these pieces stopped in the early 1960s.

The Jallar Paidar (The Jallar with Feet)

The *jallar paidar,* virtually always knotted and piled, is an ornament which was placed inside the *yurt* over the doorway. The 'feet' which were one either side of the door way are usually pointed and have wool, silk or artificial silk tassels. Wool fringes of red, indigo and alternating bands of red and indigo normally hang from the underside of the *jallar paidar.* The designs are varied and these are still being made in most parts of Afghan Turkestan, especially in the Kunduz, Mazar and Aq Chah areas. (See Colour Plate 8).

The Jallar

The *jallar* is a long narrow bag affixed to the *yurt* wall, and belongs to the category of bags loosely referred to as 'tent bags'. It is either knotted and piled or flat woven, and nearly always has woollen fringes hanging from the lower edge. (See Colour Plates 9 and 10).

Traditionally, these are made by all Turkomans (but no longer by the Yamouds and Tekkes of Herat); some are made by Uzbeks in the Maimana area. Designs of the knotted and piled *jallars* vary; the flat-woven *jallars* usually display the *bastani gul*. What is confusing is that among many Ersari Turkomans, the knotted and piled tent bag is referred to as a *jallar* and the flat-woven bag as a *torbah* or *qaqmai torbah*. *Torbah bastani* is yet another common appellation, and has come into being because most of these pieces have the *bastani* design, which means 'enclosed'. This design does remind one of wire netting!

The Bolesht

The *pushti* or *bolesht* is a small knotted and piled bag used as a cushion or pillow. In Afghan Turkestan this bag is made in small quantities only by the weavers of Andkhoy.

The Torbah

The *torbah* is another type of 'tent bag' of varying size, but squarer and smaller than the *jallar*. It is also either knotted and piled or flat woven; some have fringes. They are made throughout Afghan Turkestan by Ersaris and also in Herat by Tekkes. (See Colour Plate 11).

The Kola-i-Chergh

This is a distinctive bag, often gaily embroidered and tasselled, made from flat-woven cloth. The *kola-i-chergh* is always made in pairs, and its purpose is to hold, when migrating, the ends of the wooden poles which make up the *yurt* structure. These bags have suffered from being miscalled, variously, water bottle holders, nosebags for horses and camel ornamentations. Made by many Ersari clans, some of these bags are embroidered in silk, a sign of both the wealth and prestige of the bride's father and family. They form part of the dowry and in the *yurt* are used for the storing of female jewellery and ornaments. (See Colour Plate 12). These tent-pole bags are also made of felt by Uzbeks and Kirghiz.

Tent Bands

One of several tent bands may be seen inside the *yurt,* looped around the wooden framework. These woollen bands provide both decoration and a support to which tent bags are attached. Lengths go up to twenty metres, with widths varying between five centimetres and thirty centimetres. The wider bands are wound around the outside of the *yurt,* which they support. They are woven, of course, on very narrow looms and comprise various designs. The Uzbeks also weave tent bands. (See Colour Plate 14).

11

Colour Plate 11 TORBAH. This fine semi-antique Tekke dowry piece was brought to Afghanistan by a family who fled the USSR during the 1930s. While mostly flat woven, there are three latitudinal lines of the design which are piled. It was suggested to the author that this tent bag was made to hold wooden spoons used in cooking.

Author's collection

12

Colour Plate 12 KOLA-I-CHERGH. Both bags, the designs of which are typical, are flat woven rectangular pieces sewn down the side, with the bottom edge puckered before joining. Tassels are then put on. The longer of the two pieces illustrated is decorated with the bastani design (see Plate 10) executed in green-yellow silk. These bags which are always made in pairs, form part of the traditional dowry. (80 x 38cm and 71 x 40cm).

Author's collection

13

Colour Plate 13 Oldish *KHOURJEEN.* The gul is associated with the Sulayman clan. It used to appear in the Andkhoy production until the mid-1960s, when it went out of fashion. However, it was resuscitated in the Aq Chah production during the latter part of the last decade. This piece, woven with yarn dyed with madder, is from Andkhoy, although the border rosette is usually associated with goods from Sheberghan. (113 x 58cm).

Author's collection

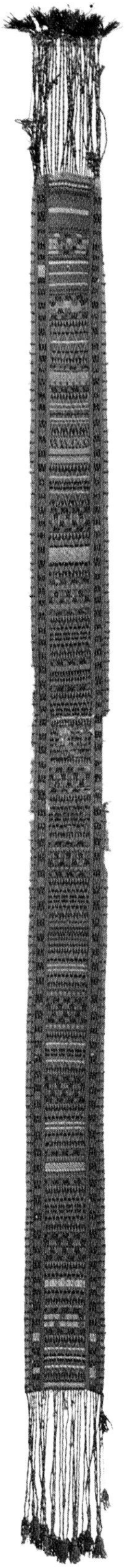

Colour Plate 14. *TENT BAND.* A Turkoman tent band. These form part of the dowry and are made in different widths. This one, approximately 18cm wide, would be for use outside the yurt. Generally speaking, the narrower ones are used inside the yurt where they have a dual purpose: holding the felt in position and also as an anchor.

Courtesy Pieter van Aalst, Breda, Holland, private collection

1

15

16

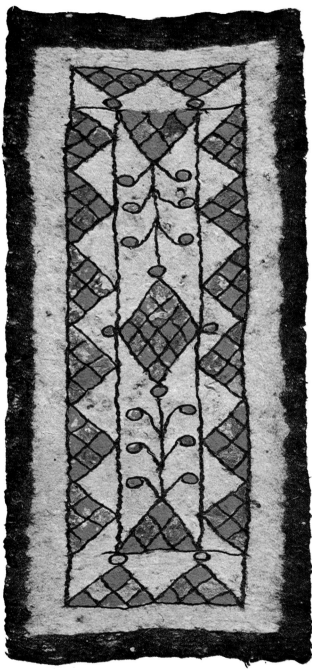

Colour Plate 16 An oldish Yamoud ASMALYK from Herat. Asmalyks, usually made in pairs, are used in decorating the flanks of camels and sometimes horses. Now extremely rare in Afghanistan. (Size 118 x 74cm at the highest point).

Colour Plate 17 A Yamoud ASMALYK. (117 x 69cm).

Colour Plate 15 A Turkoman NAMAD. Because of the flowered pattern, often referred to as gul-i-namad. *(In India and Pakistan, these felts are called namdas.) (191 x 95cm).*

17

The Namak Donneh

The *namak donneh,* or 'salt bag', is a very small *torbah,* nearly always flat woven, which often has a geometric design woven into the fabric (see page 53).

The Khourjeen

The *khourjeen* is a bag made in joined pairs, either knotted and piled or flat woven. It is often called a 'donkey bag', though it is usually carried by a man over the shoulder, and is not a dowry piece, being made by the new bride after marriage. These bags are made throughout Afghan Turkestan and also form an important part of the Beluch and Beluch-type production. (See Colour Plate 13).

The Salanchak or Gaz

This woven piece is a cradle, and is often made by the bride's mother-in-law. Among the Turkomans, it is usually knotted and piled; made by the Uzbek and Arabis, it is often flat woven. It, too, does not form part of the dowry, but is usually made and donated by the groom's mother in time for the birth of her grandchild.

Carpets and Rugs

The first carpet and rug in the Turkoman *yurt* were always dowry pieces. The making of these pieces was a labour of love as well as of prestige. Particular care and diligent patience were taken in both the sorting and the carding of the finest quality wool, invariably the spring clip. One sees in these old works of art a variety of colour and details in design which are lacking in much of current commercial production. Among the poorer families owning only a few sheep, the finest wool destined for these dowry pieces would be saved up from one year to the next.

Namads

Turkoman *namads* or felt rugs were, and are, traditionally made from the autumn clip. The felting process is usually done by women. The sheared wool is spread out on a reed mat and a lateral strip is sprinkled with boiling water and then rolled up as tightly as possible. The women work on their knees, vigorously rolling and unrolling the dampened section with the underside of their forearms until the whole is felted. Often these *namads* are decorated, and are then called *gul donneh,* or 'flowered pieces'. Different coloured wool is also placed in a pattern on the fibres being felted, which becomes integrated into the fabric and the design, which is usually very crude, is thus permanently fixed. A fairly recent development is the 'Uzbek' *namad* made in and near Mazar. These black felt appliqué fabrics have crude and vivid designs embroidered in artificial silk or cotton. (See Colour Plate 15).

Animal Trappings

Apart from the *khourjeens* and *salanchak,* other Turkoman pieces not part of the dowry may include the *asmalyk,* a five-sided knotted and piled trapping which comes to a slight point at the top. Extremely rare in Afghanistan today,

Turkoman jewellery

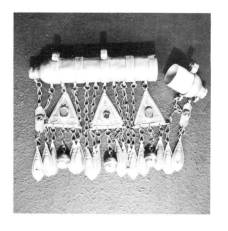

Turkoman breastplate. Verses from the holy Koran are placed inside the cylinder

these are used as decoration on the flanks of the camel transporting the bride to her new home. (See Colour Plates 16, 17 and 18).

The camel head-dress, also rare, was made of tightly plaited gold coloured wool, and was often ornamented with small mirrors or coloured glass to reflect the sun. Knotted and piled knee-caps with small bells for either horses or camels are seldom made these days, and the custom is to borrow them from a neighbour when the need arises, as with the camel head-dress. (See Colour Plate 19).

A poor Turkoman's wedding procession

The *zin-i-asp* or saddle cloth, with a slit for the pommel, and the horse blanket with the underside of felt and covered with a flat-woven material in narrow bands of bright colours and a small design, are other animal trappings that are still being made (See Colour Plate 20).

More and more Turkomans are abandoning their traditional *yurts* in favour of flat-roofed, brick houses. Many of the erstwhile traditional items are, therefore, no longer being made. The *purdah*, for example, formerly a significant element in the furnishings of a Turkoman *yurt*, is no longer being made for its original purpose. However, as todays *purdahs* form an important part of Afghan carpets, they merit a separate section (see page 56).

Non-Turkoman Tent Furnishings

Among other non-Turkoman peoples, namely Beluch, and other semi-nomads who live in either *chaparis*, a round felt-covered tent not unlike a *yurt*, or in the traditional black goat hair tent referred to as the 'bedouin' tent, furnishings and receptacles are made to fit their particular way of life.

The Mafraj

In northern Afghanistan, the *mafraj* is mainly made by Uzbeks, particularly around Mazar and Tashkurghan and is a long, narrow bag, smaller than the *jallar*. The *mafraj*, which is always knotted and piled, displays the typical geometric *gul* of the Uzbeks. It is generally used by women for the storage of their personal belongings. (See Colour Plate 21).

The Boleshts

The Beluch and other tribes, including some Pashtuns now settled in the north of Afghanistan who make Beluch-type goods, weave a large rectangular bag called a *bolesht*, or pillow. This measures approximately 1 x .60m and the face is knotted and piled, with a flat woven back, which may be decorated with bands of colour. The opening is at the narrow side. (See Colour Plates 22 and 23).

The Torbah

This smaller rather square bag in varying sizes is extensively used. Some bags are knotted and piled, though the majority are flat woven with a small repetitive design; some are partly knotted and piled and partly flat woven. Many of these bags are heavily decorated with tassels, pompoms, snail or cowrie shells, countless white buttons and small round mirrors. The mirrors used today are sometimes the lids of Afghan snuff tins, imported in large quantities from Hong Kong. (See Colour Plates 24 and 25).

18

19

Colour Plate 18 Ersari Turkoman CAMEL COVERING used for weddings. This piece is slung over the dromedary's hump, the kilim side nearest to the animal's neck. On the piled part is placed a wooden platform — sometimes a charpai *bed — on which the bride, bedecked in jewellery and wearing her finest garments, will be escorted to the home of the groom. (Overall size 145 x 83cm, piled area 96 x 61cm).*

Colour Plate 19 Ersari Turkoman CAMEL HEAD-DRESS. The top part is made of horse's hair, from the tail or mane. Primarily made of wool, they are highly ornamented with pompoms predominantly in yellow or gold, and are handed down from family to family.

20

Colour Plate 20 ZIN-I-ASP — saddle cloth. This piece was made in Qala-i-Zal and depicts the Beshiri boteh *design. Note the deep maroon red which is typical of the production from the Kunduz region. The slit is made and sited to house the pommel, and the selvedge is made of horsehair. Saddle cloths do not form part of the dowry. Older pieces are frequently damaged, the result of a fold formed whilst in use. (66 x 36cm).*

20a

Colour Plate 20a A semi-antique BESHIR rug depicting the boteh *design and woven in Kunduz Province. Both the open field and the straight transverse bands are somewhat unusual; more often they slant downwards from the vertical spring (see Colour Plate 20). While variations of this* boteh *design are not uncommon, this particular interpretation appears to have been discontinued circa 1950, though now resuscitated in refugee camps. The field is of an unusual soft brick-rose; the dyestuff used could be rang-i-dokhtar (literally, colour of the maiden), a dye also used as a cosmetic. (Circa 1940; 176 x 107cm).*

Shir Khosrow Paiwand

Colour Plate 21 Uzbek *MAFRAJ (small tent bag).* *(114 x 37cm).*

21

22

23

Colour Plate 22 Oldish Beluch-type BOLESHT. *The horsehair loops at the top end are for fastening. These are used as cushions in tents as well as in permanent dwellings. (99 x 65cm).*

Author's collection

Colour Plate 23 Oldish Beluch BOLESHT. (93 x 64cm).
Author's collection

24a

Colour Plate 24a A pair of very fine Beluch kilim TORBAHS of extraordinary precision. These two pieces (one showing the back, from which the fineness of the weave can be appreciated), woven with hand-spun yarn, are undoubtedly dowry pieces and come from the Chakhansur district. These tent bags date from circa 1930; the tassels are a more recent addition. (62 x 35cm; 61 x 36cm).

Shir Khosrow Paiwand

24

25

Colour Plate 25. Nomadic kilim *TORBAH. This type of tent bag is placed on the back of the camel when the clan is on the move. Quite often nomadic* torbahs *are part* kilim *and part pile. (52 x 65cm).*

2

Colour Plate 24 Nomadic TORBAH (tent bag) of the Beluch-type production. This bag is half pile and half kilim. *The back is entirely flat weave and is decorated with bands of varying width and different colours. Note the horsehair loops which are interlaced when closing. (55 x 55cm).*

Author's collection

Colour Plate 26 Semi-antique Beluch NAMAK DONNEH (salt bag) from the Farah area in South-West Afghanistan. Both the face and reverse side are knotted and piled; the neck is somewhat longer than usual. (64 x 33cm).

Collection of R. Stewart, Esq.

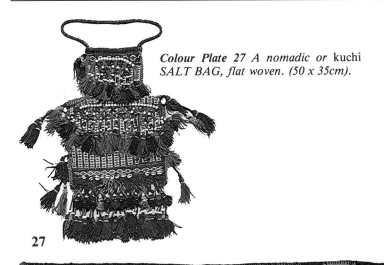

Colour Plate 27 A nomadic or kuchi *SALT BAG, flat woven. (50 x 35cm).*

27

28

29

Colour Plate 28 Embroidered kilim *SALT BAG*. The obverse side is a series of bands of different colours and widths varying from 1 to 8cm. This much decorated piece was made near Karokh, some twenty miles north of Herat city, in Taimani country. Both the shape (the shorter neck) and the intricate needlework pattern suggest that the maker had become entirely sedentary. (53 x 43cm).

Collection of P. Burke, Esq.

Colour Plate 29 The PUL DONNEH, or money bag, now very rare in Afghanistan. A genuine Beluch piece. (90 x 20cm).

Collection of P.R.J. Ford, Esq.

30

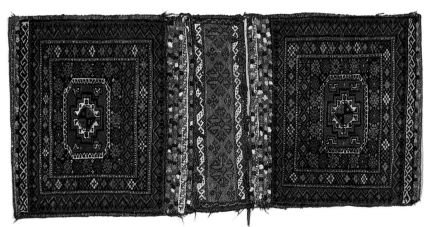

Colour Plate 30 Beluch KHOURJEEN. The brightly coloured pompoms are typical of both piled and flat-woven goods which are made in Afghan Beluch country, i.e. the western frontier area south of Herat city. (108 x 50cm).

Author's collection

31

Colour Plate 31 *Wool embroidered DASTERKHAN or eating cloth. A black or dark brown woollen fabric embroidered with either coloured wool, cotton or artificial silk, these pieces are made especially by the Sunni Hazaras of the Qala-i-Nau district, who are one of the Chahar Aimaqs. (231 x 69cm).*

32

Colour Plate 32 *Artificial silk embroidered DASTERKHAN (eating cloth). The black or dark brown woollen fabric is very typical of the N.W. part of Afghanistan. This is a particularly ornate example; most are far simpler in design and the embroidery is done with coloured wool. (198 x 68cm).*

The Namak Donneh

The Beluch *namak donneh,* or salt bag, becoming scarcer every year, is of a very different shape from that of the Turkoman. The neck of this container is narrow, yet just wide enough to pull out a handful of rock salt. This shape obviously reduces waste. Knotted and piled salt bags are rare; flat-woven salt bags are nearly always decorated with small repetitive patterns, similar to the *torbah.* They are often embellished with tassels or shells. (See Colour Plates 26, 27 and 28).

The Pul Donneh

The *pul donneh,* or money bag, is very rare nowadays. It is a long narrow bag measuring about 90 x 20cm, and only flat-woven examples of these have appeared in recent years. (See Colour Plate 29).

The Khourjeen

The *khourjeen,* a double bag which can be either flat woven or knotted and piled, performs much the same function as does a basket in Western countries. A larger version used as panniers on donkeys is also made. This type of bag is often referred to as a 'donkey bag' even though the smaller versions are used by humans. (See Colour Plate 30).

The Dasterkhan

The *dasterkhan,* or eating cloth, is made in two shapes. The long and narrow ones vary in size and are flat woven, often with narrow stripes of black and white wool and a border design different from the end design.

A larger model is made by the Aimaqs to the north of Herat, of a flimsy woollen fabric or undyed natural dark brown wool. A small rectangular design or a large concentric diamond embroidered with wool of different pastel shades are common. A variant of this larger cloth is made near Qala-i-Nau by Aimaqs and is embroidered overall in artificial silk, but these decorative pieces are made entirely for commercial sale.

A square eating cloth, usually of two pieces of flat-woven fabric sewn up the middle, with a knotted and piled band in constrasting colours, is made by the Taimanis, east of Herat. (See Colour Plates 31 and 32).

Beluch and Beluch-type Animal Trappings

Trappings for horses and camels are more varied than those made by the Turkomans, probably due to the wider range of ethnic groups.

The Beluch camel head-dress of flimsy plaited purple wool is neither as attractive nor as durable as that used at Turkoman weddings. However, camel neck-bands, to which are often attached a camel bell, range from the colourful though coarse pieces woven in the province of Ghor to the sombre yet fine piled goods from Adraskhan in Farah Province. (See Colour Plates 33, 34, 35 and 36).

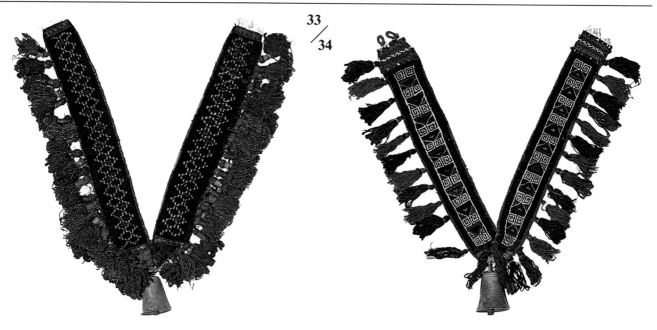

33

34

35

36

Colour Plate 33 Beluch CAMEL NECK-BAND with bell. The very fine weave and dark colours are typical of goods made in the Chakhansur region of S.W. Afghanistan. Each arm measures 80 x 13cm.

Colour Plate 34 CAMEL NECK-BAND with bell. Each arm measures 108 x 50cm.

Colour Plate 35 A Beluch NECK-BAND for donkey. The bell is of the shape often used on rams. (185 x 74cm).

Colour Plate 36 Two views of a Beluch CAMEL HEAD-DRESS.

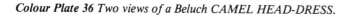

37

Colour Plate 37 *A KELDAR PURDAH of Sulayman weave. Note the* badam gul *(the 'almond' design — sometimes described as the man with two wives) embroidered in the* kilim. *This feature is a hallmark of the Sulayman production from this town. (216 x 163cm).*

Author's collection

Storage Bags

Large woollen mesh bags, sometimes decorated with coloured pompoms and tassels, as well as mirrors, are common among the Pushtu-speaking nomads. These stretchable bags are used for storing food, especially melons in season, and for other household items when on the move.

Of all the pieces described above, those still being made in Afghanistan today, either for dowry pieces or for sale, include:

purdahs, carpets and rugs
juwals, boleshts, jallars, jallar paidars, torbahs, salt bags, *khourjeens*
and *mafraj*
kilims
namads
tent bands
saddle cloths, horse blankets and various other animal trappings.

The Purdah

The special carpet with its unmistakable design which was used solely as a closure to a *yurt* is called *purdah,* or curtain, in Afghanistan. In the USSR, it is called *ensi* and in Iran, generally, *hatchlu.*

This carpet has a fringe at the bottom and a cord at each corner, sometimes of goat hair, at the top for tying to the wooden frame of the *yurt.* The *purdah* design has become very popular and is now also executed in carpet form, that is, larger than the traditional *purdah* of the *yurt,* and with fringes at both ends.

The overall design usually consists of a wide vertical and horizontal band in the form of a cross separating the centre field into four panels. Following the old tradition, each panel usually displays the candlestick motif in one of its many interpretations. In new Afghan pieces, the secondary motifs in both borders and ends often denote the clan to which the weaver belongs.

Though significantly absent in old pieces, in many *purdahs* the two segments of the vertical band come to a point, suggestive of a *mihrab,* or prayer niche. It is this that may have given rise to the belief that *purdahs* were used as prayer mats. Although opinions are divided, the author's view is that it was most unlikely that a *purdah* was a dual-purpose carpet. Apart from the sheer tedium of untying and retying the *purdah* five times a day, it is difficult to believe, even assuming that the *yurts* are pitched away from the prevailing winds, that the interior would be left exposed to the frequent and violent sand and wind storms while the inhabitants make their devotions on the front door. Moreover, I have never met a Turkoman who admitted to saying his prayers on a *purdah.* It is far more probable that the appearance of this so-called *mihrab,* now so common, was the result of a normal evolution of this art — perhaps inspired by the weaver's piety. Some say that the cross is a reproduction of a wooden door panel. There is not much credence to this theory as most *yurt* doors have no panels.

Purdahs are woven by Ersari Turkomans in large parts of Afghan Turkestan, though only very rarely in Daulatabad and Andkhoy. The finest *purdahs* undoubtedly come from Keldar, a small town on the Amu Darya River due north of Tashkurghan, and it is probably the *purdahs* woven by the Sulayman clan which take pride of place. For quite a while, most of the Keldar production was sold in Mazar and bought up by a single dealer. Today, a small though constant supply can be found in the Kabul market, where many pieces are 'antiqued', that is chemically treated or sun faded. The Keldar *purdahs* display the *chodor gul,* a flattened diamond containing nine small motifs, in the borders, the ends, and also in the horizontal band. Gold, white, indigo and

Sulayman purdah

various shades of red are used, and green in the *guls* is also common. The *purdahs* woven by the Sulaymans invariably have a finely integrated *badam gul,* or almond flower, in the *kilim* at the fringed end. (See Colour Plate 37).

The Qala-i-Zal *purdahs* from the Kunduz area come next in order of fineness. A characteristic of these carpets is squares of different colours embroidered on the *kilim.* (See pages 100 and 101, and Colour Plate 43). Moreover, the reds are the deep bluey-reds associated with the Kunduz production. The most prolific *purdah* weavers in this area are the Dalis and the Chaii. The Dalis nearly always portray the comb motif at one or both ends, and the Chaii a continuous band of cross-like motifs in white bordering the field.

Purdahs from Mazar and its surrounding areas are woven by several Ersari Turkoman clans, but the most common designs are those of the Mazar Delis. The reds of these Mazar Dali *purdahs* are brighter than the Kunduz Dalis, although ten years ago they were virtually indistinguishable.

Several different *purdahs* are made in the Aq Chah region. The Chakesh clan *purdah* is among the most easily recognisable. It always has its typical motif at one end. (See Colour Plate 38).

The Taghan clan nearly always introduces the star and/or the trefoil motif in the borders or ends. Older pieces portray the 'tree design'. (See Colour Plate 39).

Finally, the Karaboiin *purdah,* as well as the Saltuq from Sheberghan, has its bold individual motif in the bottom end. (See Colour Plate 40).

A growing tendency to eliminate white is noticeable in this wide range of *purdahs* made in Aq Chah. This is in response to European taste which feels that too much white makes for fussiness. Variations in traditional designs are also beginning to appear. One innovation is two vertical and two horizontal bands instead of only one; another is the production of mat-sized *purdahs* with an overall candlestick motif.

Stylised versions of this traditional design are also being woven outside of Afghan Turkestan in both Qaisar and Tchitchaktu by members of non-Turkoman tribes. In Herat, a more classical version of the *purdah* design is woven by Tekke Turkomans.

Purdah Characteristics:

General: Since *purdahs* are woven over extended areas of Afghanistan by various clans of Ersari Turkomans, and others, characteristics cannot be generalised. Double wefted.

Design: Unique *purdah* design, with variations in border and field details. Generally synthetic dyes (some natural dyes in Herat, Qaisar and Qala-i-Zal). Traditionally all Karaqul wool. *Kilims,* various.

Colours: Predominantly synthetic red, indigo; white; in Kunduz area also synthetic gold, orange and green. The Qala-i-Zal *purdahs* are traditionally in very deep and sombre colours.

Warps: 3-ply Karaqul wool, undyed.

Wefts: 2-ply Karaqul wool, dyed red.

Selvedges: Karaqul wool, usually dyed indigo; blanket stitch. Often bound with goat hair. Old pieces have flat goat hair selvedge.

Knots: Asymmetric, i.e. Persian or Senneh.

Sizes: Sizes vary, generally between 2.5m^2 and 4m^2.

Serai

39a

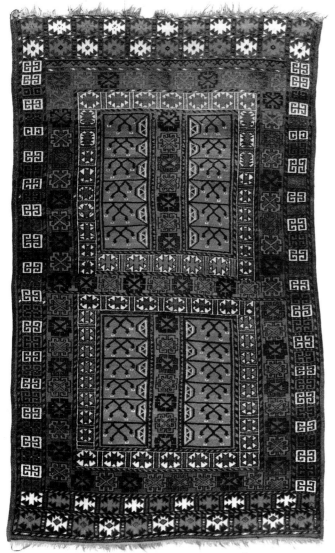

39b

Colour Plate 39a An old CHAII PURDAH from the Mazar-i-Sherif district. A distinguishing feature of this production is the double row of geometric elongated rosette motifs which appears on both skirts as well as encasing the two central panels. This motif in white often appears as a border, giving a rather jarring effect. The ground colouring is a mixture of madder and pomegranate; the selvedges are of goat hair. (Circa 1930; 220 x 130cm).

Shir Khowrow Paiwand

Colour Plate 39b An old TAGHAN PURDAH made in Taghan-Labijar. Not only is there much pale indigo throughout, but also some green in the central traverse and vertical spine. Flecks of gold (from the sparak flower) irregularly placed serve to highlight the overall richness of the colouring. Goat hair selvedges. (Circa 1920; 210 x 140cm).

Shir Khosrow Paiwand

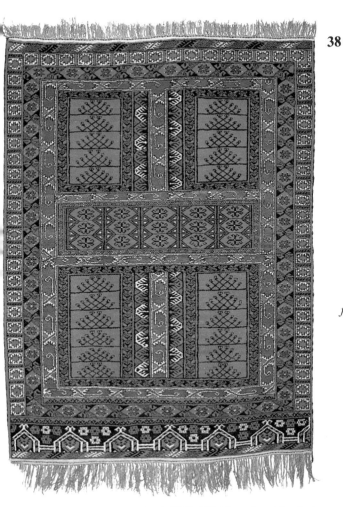

Colour Plate 39
Oldish TAGHAN
PURDAH. The
'tree' motif which
features prominently
in this piece, is
peculiar to the
Taghan production.
The 'star' motif is
also another symbol
with strong Taghan
associations. (198 x
124cm).

Colour Plate 38 CHAKESH PURDAH. Note the white design
on a dark blue ground which is on the bottom skirt. This
Chakesh motif appears only on purdahs *and* jallars — *never*
on carpets and rugs. (225 x 170cm).

Colour Plate 40 An oldish KARABOIIN PURDAH.
The most distinguishing feature of this piece is the
single wide band containing the dyrnak gul *which is so*
typical of the Karaboiins, a sub-clan very close to the
Chakesh (see Colour Plate 60). Note the two vertical
motifs which divide the field; these are very typical of
the Aq Chah production. The central lateral band
does remind one of the Saltuq production. (204 x
150cm).
Courtesy Herr H. Engelhardt, Mannheim, West Germany

Chapter 5
The Carpet Bazaar in Afghanistan

Aq Chah

Carpet bazaar

An Up-Country Bazaar

Every town of any significance in Afghanistan has its own market days, usually held twice a week, where both local and itinerant merchants, with their specialised wares, and craftsmen and artisans congregate. But only in the carpet-producing areas does each town have a section devoted entirely to carpets and related activities. This is the ever-fascinating 'Carpet Bazaar'.

The character and function of a carpet bazaar depends, of course, on the quality and the type of goods marketed there. The role and importance of a particular bazaar in a carpet-producing region can fluctuate; for instance, in recent years the bazaar of Tchitchaktu has expanded greatly, whilst that of Daulatabad has diminished.

Aq Chah, the centre of a vast carpet producing area, has the largest bazaar in Afghan Turkestan. It is situated in the main street and is held bi-weekly, on Mondays and Thursdays. Soon after dawn on these two days, villagers from all around begin to make their way towards the town. Some come on foot, others on donkey or camel, sometimes riding two or even three astride, often with rolled carpets behind them. Caravans of camels, their panniers bulging with chopped straw, melons or other seasonal produce from outlying villages, are led by their caravaneer, riding a donkey and often also bearing a rug to be sold.

As the momentum gathers, a vitality spreads through the bazaar. There is no sense of rush, however; people move with dignity and calm. From far and near, the peasants are gathering to participate in an essential and traditional social event, for that is undoubtedly what bazaar day is. Some men have come to sell home-made products, ranging from a bag of yogurt (locally called *mast)* to a ball of wool, a goat to a basket of eggs; others to buy a supply of green tea or a hand-forged hoe. A few have come simply to gossip, to enjoy the fun of bargaining, or only to stare longingly at some object quite out of their financial reach. Whatever their reason for being there, they all participate in some way and contribute to the movement, colour and atmosphere which is such an integral part of a bazaar.

The animals are tethered in the courtyard of a *serai*, the inn of the ancient world, the rooms of which are rented as warehouse space by the merchants. In the centre is a raised platform, often used as the prayer ground. In one corner is a well and in another the latrines. Whilst the merchants are transacting business in the market, the animals are fed and watered by an attendant. There is always someone at hand to collect the manure to be used as fuel, after it has been made into flat, round cakes and dried in the sun.

In the carpet section of the bazaar, next to each other, are the various dealers and buyers, all eager and ready to do business. They wait expectantly outside their shops, with impassive expressions on their faces. By seven o'clock, the area is already crowded with vendors and onlookers, all wearing the traditional Turkoman turban and multicoloured long-sleeved *chapan*. (See Frontispiece).

Most vendors, carrying their rolled-up carpet or displaying the smaller pieces, stand by and warily observe one or two sales to learn the state of the market before offering their own goods for sale.

The buyer's attitude is brisk, for there is no time to waste on lengthy haggling. A carpet is rejected immediately if its quality is not acceptable. However, if the item is of interest, it is rolled out on the earth sidewalk (there are no pavements in Aq Chah) where it is measured by an assistant using a graduated steel rule, and further appraised by the buyer.

Carpet bazaar

The asking price is invariably higher than that finally agreed upon. The abacus clicks away, though during the last two or three years battery-powered calculating machines have become popular. After a short discussion, the transaction is closed. This is signified by both parties jointly holding the cash and giving three upward shakes of the hand, followed by a final slap of hands. The carpet is then folded and stacked with the others, and the buyer turns his attention to the next offer. The seller fades into the crowd, with either a disgruntled expression or a barely concealed smirk on his face. If no agreement is reached, he will approach another buyer and the process begins all over again.

In the case of a vendor having already contracted with a dealer for the sale of his goods, the business operation is a short one. The goods are inspected and, if satisfactory, accepted. There is no bargaining as the price has previously been agreed upon.

If haggling or discussion of a price is taking too long or seems to be reaching an impasse, a self-appointed arbiter from the crowd steps in to mediate. This traditional method of accepting outside help to conclude a deal is an excellent example of the eastern philosophy regarding the importance of 'saving face'. In these cases, the arbiter hopes to find a solution acceptable to both parties, and, if successful, he steps away with this prestige further enhanced.

It sometimes happens, of course, that a vendor has set his sights too high. He will not come down in price and has refused the intervention of an arbiter or, because of the unbridgeable gap in price, no arbiter has offered his services. There is then no option for the vendor but to return home again with his rolled-up carpet on the back of his donkey. At least he will have another chance on the next bazaar day.

When negotiating the sale of a large or very fine carpet, if both parties want to maintain some degree of secrecy, they resort to the old and familiar 'code' system. One of the men grasps the other's hand hidden within the long sleeve of his *chapan*. A squeeze of his thumb means 1000 afs. each squeeze of the other fingers 100 afs. (In 1978 £1.00 was worth 85 afs.) This can be quite a performance when an arbiter is also participating.

In the bazaar, both immediate cash payment and credit are customary, though if a carpet is bought on credit, the purchase price can be up to ten per cent higher. In the bazaars of Afghan Turkestan, there exists a strong tradition of trust, rarely betrayed, which facilitates business transactions considerably.

On non-market days, the purchased carpets are remeasured, listed and baled, and prepared for shipment by lorry to the buyer's own warehouse or that of his principal in Kabul, from where the goods are exported.

Not far from the carpet bazaar in Aq Chah is the wool bazaar. During the spring and autumn, when shearing takes place, raw wool in the form of fleece is offered for sale by weight. The scales, no different from many found elsewhere in Afghanistan, are quite rudimentary. They consist of two pans, suspended from either end of a stout stick, with the operator's arm acting as fulcrum. The weights are often stones, or bits of metal from a broken gear-box or a combination of such objects. Nonetheless, the weights are accurate, adding up to one *seer,* the equivalent of seven kilos (the weight of a *seer* varies in other areas of Afghanistan).

Wool bazaar

Livestock market on bazaar day

Blowing into the incision on the goat's leg, to separate the skin from the flesh

Preparing the carcass

In the wool bazaar also congregate the dealers in goat hair (which is used primarily for making the nomad's black tent) and in dags, the hard manure-clotted parts of the fleece. There are people who earn their living by patiently breaking down these clots with a stone, separating the wool and *kemp* which is then sold for making felt.

Nearby are the merchants who sell undyed spun wool, usually in balls, but sometimes in skeins. On examination, the wide range in quality, both of the wool itself as well as the spinning, is apparent. The most expensive wool is the finely spun Karaqul used for the warp threads.

In another section of the bazaar are the professional dyers, their arms stained blue with indigo.

The livestock market, where horses, camels, sheep and goats are sold, is another animated area of the bazaar. It is one of the barometers by which the state of the local economy can be measured. The overall condition of the animals, the briskness of business and the prices obtained are all indicative of the current market conditions. Knowledge and appreciation of this 'barometer' is invaluable for, say, a visiting buyer from Kabul, in order to establish a deeper rapport with the local Turkomans.

Adjacent to the livestock market is the area where the animals are slaughtered, and their carcasses dressed. The speed and skill with which the professional slaughterers operate is quite remarkable.

After its legs are tied, the animal is placed with its head towards Mecca over a trench some forty-five centimetres deep. The jugular vein is severed with a finely honed knife and the blood let to run into the trench. Immediately after the first spurt of blood, the animal loses consciousness and is soon dead. The process is painless and has followed the injunctions of the Holy Koran.

In the case of sheep and goats, a small incision is subsequently made in the skin just above the hock of one of the hind legs. The slaughterer, or an apprentice, firmly grasps the leg in both hands and blows vigorously and directly into the incision, until the skin slowly begins to separate from the flesh. Soon the animal swells into a bloated and grotesque form, its legs sticking out stiffly from the balloon-shaped body. It is then hung by its hind legs from a tripod and its head is severed.

The skin is cut around the rear hooves, and it is but a matter of moments before the skin has been peeled off whole from the carcass. (After curing, the skin is used as a water-carrying bag or as a butter churn.

The animal is disembowelled, the heart, liver and lights are neatly placed on the severed head, next to which are placed the two front hooves, later to be joined by the rear ones.

The skin is then replaced on to the carcass by merely pulling it up and over the neck and up to the rear legs. The carcass is then taken down from the tripod, and after the rear hooves are severed, is laid on the ground to await the owner's collection after payment of a small fee.

Not all slaughtering is carried out by professionals, however. Most homes in the Afghan countryside — especially those in the mountains — will keep a wether lamb which is especially fattened for home consumption. It will be slaughtered in the late autumn of its second year, and as much as possible of the meat will be stored for consumption during the long, cold and hard winter when villages and hamlets are often cut off from the outside world for months at a time. One method of curing the flesh is to cut it into largish chunks, salt, it, and spike the pieces on to a wooden skewer. The meat is covered with muslin or a similar material, and the wooden pole is then hung horizontally in the shade to dry. When the meat has hardened it is totally cured. The fat tail is rendered and stored in earthenware pots.

The Kabul Carpet Bazaar

What is called the Kabul Carpet Bazaar is made up of three distinct components, namely, the wholesale market, the retail market, and the ancillary trades and crafts. Although undoubted changes in the character of the first two have taken place during the last five years, it is the wholesale market that has altered the most.

Facing the stadium, the adjacent playing fields and the open hills beyond, is a long, uninterrupted line of two-storeyed buildings which runs the entire length of the Chaman Khuzuri, a broad street in the east of Kabul. Here are located the exporters, middlemen, brokers, and dealers, their warehouses and their shops. Upstairs are also the rooms occupied by Turkomans and Uzbeks from the north, visiting Kabul to conduct business.

Looking south to Kabul

In the early 1970s, there were only six carpet exporters of any significance in Kabul, and four of them had their warehouses in the Chaman Khuzuri. Here they transacted all the business of buying, measuring, listing and packing. Each of them had his own 'collectors' or middlemen, who brought him the merchandise in which he specialised. As space in their warehouses was cramped, especially before a shipment, buyers were often obliged to appraise the larger carpets outside on the pavement. This would always draw a circle of curious idlers or of aimlessly wandering tourists savouring this colourful scene. Donkeys with bulging panniers of fruit, cyclists and pedestrians all about their business, exercised their right of way and nonchalantly walked across the carpets in question, frustrating the appraisal or measuring at hand. In the street, Hazara porters pulled their *karachis,* those crude flat two-wheeled carts, heaped with bales of carpets just unloaded from lorries from the north, or with goods to be taken from one buyer to another. Single Turkomans, or Uzbeks, or others, with a rug draped over their shoulders, hawked their goods up and down the street. There were no secrets; everyone knew what his competitor was up to. When business was slack, people dropped in for a chat, and over the inevitable little bowl of green tea, covetous eyes would dart around the stock in the room. The heat, multitudinous flies, inane comments from the idle watchers, in addition to the very real strain of concentrated bargaining, was a heavy price to pay for this romantic atmosphere.

After the carpet boom of 1972 and 1973, activity in the world market slackened considerably and business at the Chaman Khuzuri immediately became more competitive. Consequently, it was necessary to have a greater degree of confidentiality. Thus, several of the large exporters moved out of this bazaar area, though still retaining their contacts there.

At about the same time, several middlemen with stock on hand decided to export in their own right. They were lucky, for the arrival of their first shipments in Hamburg and London coincided with a slight upsurge in world demand. Not only did they make a profit, but they also established their first contacts abroad, and it was not long before they began travelling to Europe on a regular basis. The success of these enterprising dealers was closely watched by others in Kabul, who promptly obtained their own licences to export. Today, there are about forty exporters in the capital with their places of business in the Chaman Khuzuri and elsewhere.

The boom of 1972 and 1973, which followed the catastrophic droughts of the two previous years, described elsewhere, caused many non-Turkomans to turn to carpet weaving. As would be expected, the number of pieces at the lower end of the quality range began to increase. Fortunately for the Afghan carpet industry, a new market was found: Jeddah. For years it had been customary for Afghan pilgrims going to Mecca to take with them a rug or prayer mat. These, they would sell in Jeddah and use the proceeds to buy

Kabul

souvenirs or simply to defray the expenses of the journey. People from all over the Islamic world would congregate in Jeddah, the port of arrival, and there was never any shortage of would-be buyers. In fact, many a Hadji has regretted not taking more rugs with him and has bemoaned the loss of potential profit.

With the assistance of the Saudi Arabian government and publicity at the Trade Fair in Jeddah, an entirely new outlet for Afghan carpets was established. This had two repercussions. Firstly, the tremendously increased use of the Bokhara design, by far the most popular in the Jeddah market of Saudi Arabia. Secondly, because of the apparent inability of the Saudis to differentiate between qualities in Afghan rugs of similar design, the cheap and lower quality pieces found a market there, while on the whole, the better grades went to Europe.

There is a growing tendency for foreign dealers in new goods to do their buying directly in Kabul. As they have to work through a broker, and often an interpreter as well, it is doubtful, however, whether there is any real advantage to be gained, particularly in view of the fact that the Kabul market is supplied from the north on a fairly regular cyclical basis. Timing is all important, and to extract any real advantage the would-be buyer should be prepared to wait patiently — maybe a full week — for the right moment.

The retail carpet shops in Kabul form the second important component of this huge dispersed market. These shops are mainly found in the newer section of the town, called Shar-i-Nau (lit. new town), and practically none of these are owned or managed by Turkomans or Uzbeks. This retail trade is almost entirely in the hands of Tajiks, Pashtuns or Hazaras, the majority of whom make up in charm, glib tongues and business psychology what they lack in veracity or any form of accurate knowledge. These tourist traps also catch foreign residents in Kabul. Unlike reliable retailers in any western city, in Shar-i-Nau an inventive mind and the ability to tell the would-be buyer just what he wants to hear, ensures that these 'sharks' sooner or later will make a 'killing'. In dimly lit shops, the air swirling with dust, the walls are hung with rugs or stacked with rolled prayer mats, which creates an atmosphere of oriental splendour. The shopkeeper at a glance can size up a foreign buyer, including the measure of his wallet. After numerous cups of tea, considerable bargaining and the flattering attention of the dealer, a happy tourist will walk out of the shop, the mesmerised but proud owner of, all too often, a defective rug which he might have bought more cheaply in any major city of Europe. Many innocent buyers mistakenly believe that age and quality are synonymous. Thus, a large part of the stock of these retail shops is artificially aged by professional 'antiquers'. If they do not sell readily, they are passed on consignment to another dealer, which gives the false impression of a busy turnover in stock. These charming rogues do much towards popularising Afghan goods, albeit at the risk of influencing wholesale prices, especially as regards genuine old pieces. The supply of these is totally inadequate to meet the demands from the hordes of tourists who descend on the bazaar, certain that buying at source will be cheaper. Little do they realise that many of these shopkeepers are often in regular telephonic contact with trade buyers in Europe, and thus are quite aware of current prices there.

The third component of the Kabul carpet market consists of the connected trades and crafts. The most important of these are the carpet repairers, some of whom work freelance in their own ateliers located around the Chaman Khuzuri. Good repair work deceives all but the most skilled and practised eye. A repairer's tools consist of a hooked knife, a tailor's flat scissors, a wire brush and needles. His workbench is a board, with hammer and nails, and his materials an assortment of coloured wool. If he is to repair a worn spot or a hole, he will nail the rug to the board to fix and expose the defect. Squatting on

Washing a carpet in the street

his haunches, he will trim the area to be repaired into a rectangular shape and, having re-established the warps, he will knot these, introduce wefts and continue the pattern with wool of matching colours. After clipping it evenly, the repaired section is consolidated by hammering, and then a wire brush is briskly applied. A well-done repair job can often only be confirmed by touch. The good repairer instinctively knows how to 'read' a pattern and continue it. The unscrupulous repairers resort to 'painting' that is, using ink or some other agent to camouflage defects such as worn areas, etc.

Immediately behind Chaman Khuzuri are the carpet stretchers, whose craft is to improve the shape of a carpet or to eradicate cockles. The main cause of cockling is due to the use of badly sorted wool or of uneven tensions in the weaving. This defect will generally reappear if the piece is inadvertently wetted, or even exposed to very humid atmospheric conditions.

According to the defect to be rectified, the carpet is fixed by its fringes or selvedges to metal pins hammered into the ground. A wooden beam underneath the carpet is raised to the required height and angle by means of a jack or other form of leverage. The carpet is then wetted and the beam raised further to attain a maximum of tautness, and the whole is left to dry evenly in the sun.

Dealers in dyestuffs, imported or locally spun yarn, sellers of hessian for packing and locally made rope, all have their places of business in and around Chaman Khuzuri, as do the 'antique fakers'. This group of men has grown in number in response to the insatiable demand for old goods. They use various methods to simulate age and wear. Placing carpets in the street for traffic to run over is one method, and a startling sight it is for any Kabul newcomer. This consolidates the knots on the back of the carpet as well as splicing the pile. The hairy back of the new carpet is rapidly smoothed down by means of a blowlamp. Washing carpets with a bleaching agent tones down the harsh colours of newly made pieces, as does simple wetting and sun bleaching. Even fringes are raked thin with a wire brush and the *kilims* are discoloured in an effort to bamboozle those people who rely on these as a test of age.

Chapter 6
The Kunduz and Mazar Production

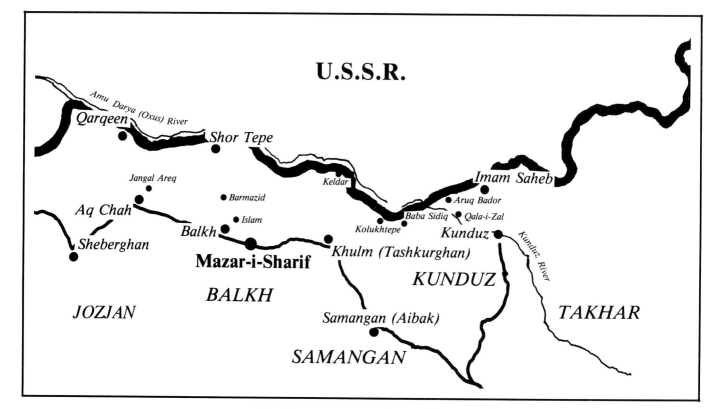

Kunduz was once a major market centre in which were sold carpets and rugs made in the three districts to the north and west of this provincial capital, namely, Imam Saheb, Qala-i-Zal and Chardarah. It has since given its name to the production from these areas, even though Kunduz itself is not, and never has been, a weaving centre, much like Bokhara in Soviet Uzbekistan which has given its name to carpets woven elsewhere but marketed there. There are, however, some three to four hundred Ersari Turkoman families of various clans living in Kunduz today, engaged in carpet weaving on a modest scale.

The opening of the paved Kunduz-Kabul road in 1964 made travel so easy that Turkomans from the Kunduz area preferred to go to the capital with even as few as two or three carpets, rather than sell them in their local bazaar. This still holds true today. Most Kunduz goods are sent directly to Kabul, with the result that Kunduz is now the smallest and least important carpet market of the four major carpet centres of Afghan Turkestan, that is, Aq Chah, Andkhoy, Mazar and Kunduz.

Kunduz, from being a malarial swamp, is now a rich agricultural area. Major irrigation and malaria control projects enabled Kunduz Province to become one of the important cotton growing areas of Afghanistan. This agricultural prosperity is being maintained at the cost of carpet production.

Today Kunduz is a thriving, animated town with tree-lined streets, the home of the Spinzar Cotton Company, a major exporter of the cotton grown in the area and a producer of edible oil and of soap. With the prevalence of Turkoman influence, Kunduz is also a foremost centre of that spectacular central Asian sport of *buzkashi*.

In the centre of town are some dozen or more shops selling carpets, rugs, *khourjeens* and old Uzbeki *kilims*. Also offered for sale are the Beluch-type *boleshts* (see Colour Plates 22 and 23), those multipurpose bags used as pillows and for storage, woven in increasing numbers by local Pashtuns. These bags tend to be a bit larger than the traditional pieces from Ghormaj or Herat, and today often contain sky-blue. The Uzbeks of this region do not make carpets, neither do other non-Turkoman tribes, with the exception of the relatively recent Pashtun production of *boleshts,* mentioned above.

Irrigated area of Kunduz plain

Imam Saheb (also called Imam Sayed)

Immam Saheb which, as its name implies, is a lieu of local pilgrimage, lies about seventy kilometres north of Kunduz, off the tarred road leading to the new port of Shirkhan on the Oxus (Amu Darya) River. The district of Imam Saheb comprises seven important villages in which live some four thousand weavers from different clans of the Ersari tribe. This area is fertile and well irrigated and thus these Turkomans do not have to depend on additional income from carpet weaving. They produce not more than 400-500m^2 per month. Most of them have abandoned their *yurts,* and live in compounds of flat-roofed mud-brick houses, and their relative prosperity is attracting Turkomans from other areas.

The original Turkoman inhabitants of Imam Saheb, established there for many generations, are of the Majar, Hassan Mangali, Dali and Taghan clans, and the finest carpets, about ten per cent of the Imam Saheb production, are in the main still being made by these clans today. Later arrivals, crossing the Oxus into Afghanistan in the 1920s, included Oumars and Ghaba Saqals (see page 123) all, of course, carpet weavers. The Ghaba Saqals who settled in Imam Saheb no longer make their traditional designs (see Colour Plate 83) but, like most of the people here, are replacing the *fil-pai,* that well-known turkoman elephant foot motif, with either the Beshiri *alma gul* (see Colour Plate 7), that is, apple blossom, or the *bagh-i-chinar gul* (the poplar leaf), (see Colour Plate 41).

Although the traditional use of natural dyestuffs has largely been abandoned in Imam Saheb, the characteristic embroidered squares of different colours on the *kilims* of carpets and rugs have to a large extent been maintained. This feature is seen in most of the Imam Saheb production and up to now is peculiar to the production from the Kunduz area as a whole, and especially to the Qala-i-Zal production.

Recently there has been a small production of pieces in which natural dyestuffs predominate, and a variety of resuscitated old designs, including the *bastani* motif, which has usually been associated with flat-woven *torbahs* and *jallars* (see page 68).

Qala-i-Zal

The *woleswali* (district headquarters) of Qala-i-Zal, some sixty kilometres north-west of Kunduz on a very rough road, is the administrative centre for seven villages, inhabited mostly by Ersari Turkomans, who are the only weavers in this area. In four of these villages, especially Kolukhtepe high on

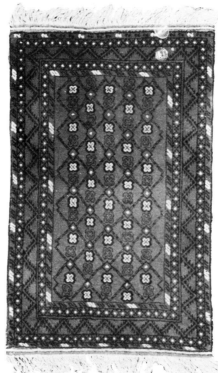

A selection of Qala-i-Zal designs, showing variations of the bastani *motif resuscitated in the late '70s.*

the infertile south banks of the Oxus (Amu Darya), the finest carpets of the Qala-i-Zal production are woven. In fact, ninety per cent of the Qala-i-Zal production falls in the First Quality category of Afghan Turkoman carpets.

In the district as a whole, traditions tend to die hard. The *yurt* is still largely used as a dwelling place, and the Turkomans way of life has changed little. Carding and spinning of wool is still entirely by hand, and the use of cotton wefts — that nefarious practice introduced in 1971 which has so altered the handle and the back of the traditional Afghan carpet — is unknown here. The price of good craftsmanship has not been compromised by base commercialism. The weavers of Qala-i-Zal work slowly and meticulously, producing maybe one or two carpets a year. (See Colour Plate 42).

Two significant changes, however, are apparent. Firstly, synthetic red dyestuffs have taken the place of madder, though Turkomans here have continued to produce the deep red, albeit synthetic, which is characteristic of the Qala-i-Zal production. Secondly, the *purdah* and Dali *fil-pai* designs as well as the square *kheshti gul* (brick *gul*) designs, which were woven almost exclusively up to the mid-1970s, have now largely been replaced by the *alma gul* and the *bagh-i-chinar gul* associated with the Beshiris. Here, as in the Imam Saheb production, the embroidered squares of colour on the *kilims* are a distinguishing feature. (See Colour Plate 43, and page 68 depicting variations and the *bastani* motif resuscitated in the late '70s).

Also made in Qala-i-Zal are piled *khourjeens* of excellent workmanship, often sombre in colour. Many of these have a piled panel joining the two bags, which is unusual for Afghan *khourjeens*.

Chardarah

The third carpet weaving area around Kunduz is Chardarah, about fifty kilometres to the west, on a rough road which passes through arid and sandy terrain before reaching this relatively fertile region. Three large Ersari villages make up this centre, each inhabited by two to three thousand Turkomans from various Ersari clans. Their numbers have recently been increased by Turkomans from Aq Chah and Andkhoy attracted by the more favourable agricultural conditions.

The majority of the Chardarah production is slightly above average in quality. Up to a few years ago, designs consisted mainly of the Qazan, Dali and Taghan *fil-pai*. The current trend is to weave the *bagh-i-chinar* and *alma gul*, as in the Qala-i-Zal and Imam Saheb production.

Kunduz Characteristics:

General: The following characteristics apply only to carpets of the first quality, of which eighty per cent of the entire Kunduz production comes from Qala-i-Zal. Firm and supple handle. Back slightly ridged. Tight knotting. Double wefted. Mostly synthetic dyes. Finest Karaqul wool; Kandahari wool for white motifs. *Kilim* nearly always with embroidered coloured squares.

Colours: Varying reds, tending to deep red-maroon. Gold/orange, indigo, green, white.

Warps: 2-ply undyed Karaqul wool.

Wefts: Generally 1-ply dark Karaqul wool.

Selvedges: Blue, red, often undyed natural wool; blanket stitch.

Knots: Persian or Senneh asymmetric.

Sizes: 200cm x 100cm, 200cm x 125cm and 300cm x 200cm.

The Qarqeen Production

Like all Turkomans, the Qarqeens are weavers, but their current production of carpets and rugs is radically different nowadays. The reason for this is simple. In former times, the Qarqeens wove almost exclusively for their domestic requirements, including, of course, those pieces needed for a dowry. (See Colour Plates 44 and 45).

However, a few of the less poor members of the community did weave larger carpets to sell. Many of these large and attractive pieces, often measuring 12m² (4.00m x 3.00m) have been exported to the West although some are still to be seen in Kabul where they grace the floors of embassies and are much admired for their beautiful, mellow colours.

The Qarqeens do not possess designs that can be said to be uniquely theirs, though for many years, the extra large *fil-pai gul* surrounded by a dotted border as seen in current Qazan and Dali pieces, with a plain rectangle in the centre of the *gul,* was a predominant feature of their production. The large Qarqeen always displayed this elephant-foot pattern. The secondary *gul* varied; sometimes the Tree of Life or the eight-star motif was incorporated between each row of *guls;* sometimes there was no secondary *gul* at all. The borders, as a rule, were not intricate, but rather bold and simple. The Bokhara *gul* never appeared, nor did any white feature.

Madder, which grows abundantly in the Shor Tepe region to the east, was widely used and blue was always from natural indigo, unlike today's production where madder is never used and chemical black takes the place of indigo. In some of the smaller dowry pieces, green and madder-rose, and also yellow appeared. Often undyed natural brown wool would highlight a motif in either the field or the border. The old Qarqeen carpet was always double wefted, with both warps and wefts of undyed Karaqul wool, the latter being loosely introduced when weaving. A distinguishing feature of these pieces was a neat back, only slightly ridged, and a very regular stitch.

Around 1958, the Qarqeens turned to the making of cheap coarse carpets on a commercial scale, generally in sizes from 7m² to 9m² and these smaller pieces, together with rugs, now constitute the bulk of today's production. They very rarely make runners or mats.

The designs used in today's production include copies of the Chakesh, Qazan and Dali *guls,* also crude versions of the *alma gul* and the Bokhara *gul.*

At least eighty per cent of the goods produced by the Qarqeens is the coarsest and cheapest produced anywhere by Turkomans in Afghanistan. The poverty of these people forces them to use the cheapest materials possible, and to get the work off the loom as fast as they can. Their policy would seem to be 'a minimum of time for a maximum return on a minimum outlay'. A weaver from Aq Chah will take thirty man-days per square metre for an average quality piece, whereas in Qarqeen, three weavers will take thirty man days to complete a carpet measuring 6m² (3.00 x 2.00m), or just half the time.

The cheapest wool, mainly Karaqul — much of it 'dead' wool from the tanning factory in Aq Chah — is sold in Qarqeen on Mondays and Thursdays when their bi-weekly bazaar is held. The cheapest chemical dyestuffs are also used in the majority of these goods.

Furthermore, it is not unusual for Qarqeen carpets to have wefts of hemp. This despicable practice is deplorable, as hemp rots quickly. A hemp weft can be detected by its smell. In addition, the spongy texture of these carpets should put the potential buyer on his guard. However, as with every rule there is an exception, and perhaps five per cent of the Qarqeens production is totally atypical and falls into the medium-fine category of Ersari Turkoman goods.

Finished pieces go to Kabul by road via Mazar. There are only four dealers in Kabul who specialise in these cheap carpets, most of which are exported to Jeddah in Saudi Arabia.

41

43

Colour Plate 41 BAG-I-CHINAR GUL. *(162 x 123cm).*
Courtesy Herr H. Engelhardt, Mannheim, West Germany

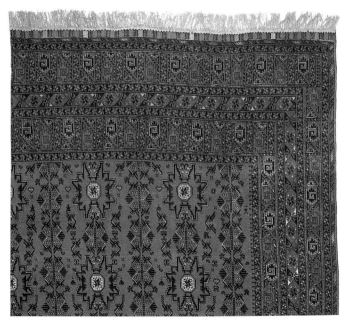

Colour Plate 43 QALA-I-ZAL *rug with a* bastani *design.
Natural dyestuffs have been used, the dark shades and
the brown from walnut peel (210 x 120cm).*

42

Colour Plate 42 Quarter of an oldish QALA-I-ZAL *carpet in a
Caucasian-type design which was relatively common until the
mid-seventies. (394 x 293cm).*

Author's collection

44 / 45

Colour Plate 44 Semi-antique QARQEEN prayer rug. Apart from natural undyed brown and white yarn, natural dyestuffs used include madder and sparak. The green is obtained by mixing sparak and indigo. (104 x 72cm).

Author's collection

Colour Plate 45 A semi-antique QARQEEN rug showing the very large fil-pai gul. (Note this piece from the design could be mistaken for an old Sulayman). (224 x 110cm).

Courtesy Pieter van Aalst, Breda, Holland

44a

Colour Plate 44a A classical old QARQEEN rug depicting an over-size Arangi gul. Typical of the old Qarqeen production — which, alas, is now discontinued — is the relative fineness of weave, the large and bold guls, simple yet strong borders and a ground colour of madder brown. The yarn is hand-spun Karaqul wool and some undyed brown yarn has been used in the border to highlight the design. (Circa 1950; 203 x 117cm).

Shir Khosrow Paiwand

Part of a ruined mosque in Balkh

Like many of the Ersari Turkomans, there are Qarqeens to be found scattered in different centres of carpet-producing areas, and the quality of their weaving tends to match the local standard wherever they may be. For instance, there are Qarqeens in such centres as Aq Chah and Mazar who produce quite acceptable work by local criteria.

Qarqeen Characteristics:

General:	Often spongy handle. Coarse hairy back; large coarse and loose knotting, double wefted. Synthetic dyes throughout, especially cheap non-indigo blue or black.
Designs:	Bokhara *gul, alma gul* and elephant foot. Cotton wefts plainly visible, very coarse Karaqul wool; often 'dead' wool. Plain undyed *kilim*.
Colours:	Red, blue/black, white.
Warps:	2- or 3-ply, undyed varied wool.
Wefts:	Usually cotton of 2- or 3-ply. If of wool, also 2- or 3-ply. Sometimes hemp wefts usually dyed red or pale blue.
Selvedges:	Red, blue or black; blanket stitch.
Knots:	Asymmetric.
Sizes:	300 x 200cm and some rugs 200 x 100cm.

The Mazar-i-Sharif Production

Mazar-i-Sharif, the fourth largest town in Afghanistan, was merely a suburb of Balkh until the late nineteenth century when, because of its more salubrious climate, it was made the capital of Balkh Province. The heart of this city in the vast arid plain of Afghan Turkestan, blown by the winds of the central Asian steppes, is the great Mosque of Ali, the most venerated shrine and lieu of pilgrimage for Shi'a Muslims in all Afghanistan (see page 21).

Balkh itself, on the old Silk Route, some twenty kilometres west of Mazar, is one of the famous ancient sites of Afghanistan, with a noble history going as far back as Achaemenid times. Zoroaster is said to have preached here. The local silversmiths produced some of the most beautiful examples of their art in the world. Alexander the Great married the legendary Roxane in this majestic northern capital, known throughout Asia as the Mother of Cities. It continued to flourish under Islamic rule until it was reduced to rubble by Genghis Khan in the early thirteenth century. Today the somnolent streets of Balkh still maintain their own particular atmosphere as they wind through the ruins and remains of their forgotten glory. One of the most striking sites is the tenth century Masjid-i-Gombad (the Mosque of Nine Domes), of which only the decorated pillars and arches remain, exquisitely carved. At the top of each pillar is a wide decorated band in which the *boteh*, or paisley leaf, figures clearly.

Although virtually no carpets are woven in the town of Mazar itself, it like Kunduz, has given its generic name to the productions from the thirteen carpet weaving districts surrounding this city, in or through which they are marketed. One notable exception is the famous Tekke carpets of Barmazid.

Barmazid

Section of the carpet bazaar in Mazar-i-Sharif

The village of Barmazid, equidistant from Balkh and Daulatabad (Balkh Province), has grown from its one hundred and thirty original houses to the

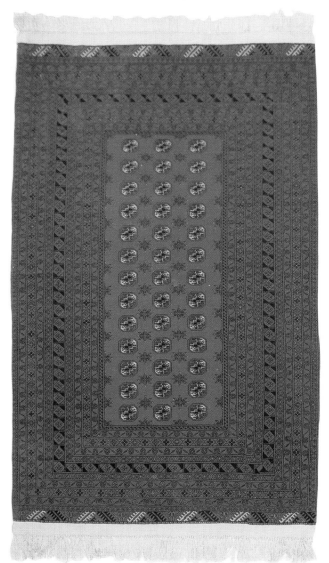

46

47

Colour Plate 46 BARMAZID. As would be expected in Tekke Turkoman pieces, both the primary and secondary Tekke guls fill the field. Another typical feature of the production is the wide border, in this example comprising twelve guards. Note the very white imported mill-spun yarn. (239 x 172cm).

Colour Plate 47 SHARKH. The similarities in design between this piece and the Barmazid (Colour Plate 46) are very obvious and to be expected, both being woven by Tekke Turkomans. Likewise, the stitch and handle are identical and distinctive, and not to be confused with a host of imitations made by non-Tekkes throughout the Turkoman carpet weaving areas of Afghanistan. (Approx. 300 x 200cm).

Colour Plate 48 BABA SIDIQ PURDAH. The bright colours used in this piece are typical, as is the blue Beshiri border. The gold and green, both essential characteristics, are not evident in the photograph. (246 x 157cm).

48a

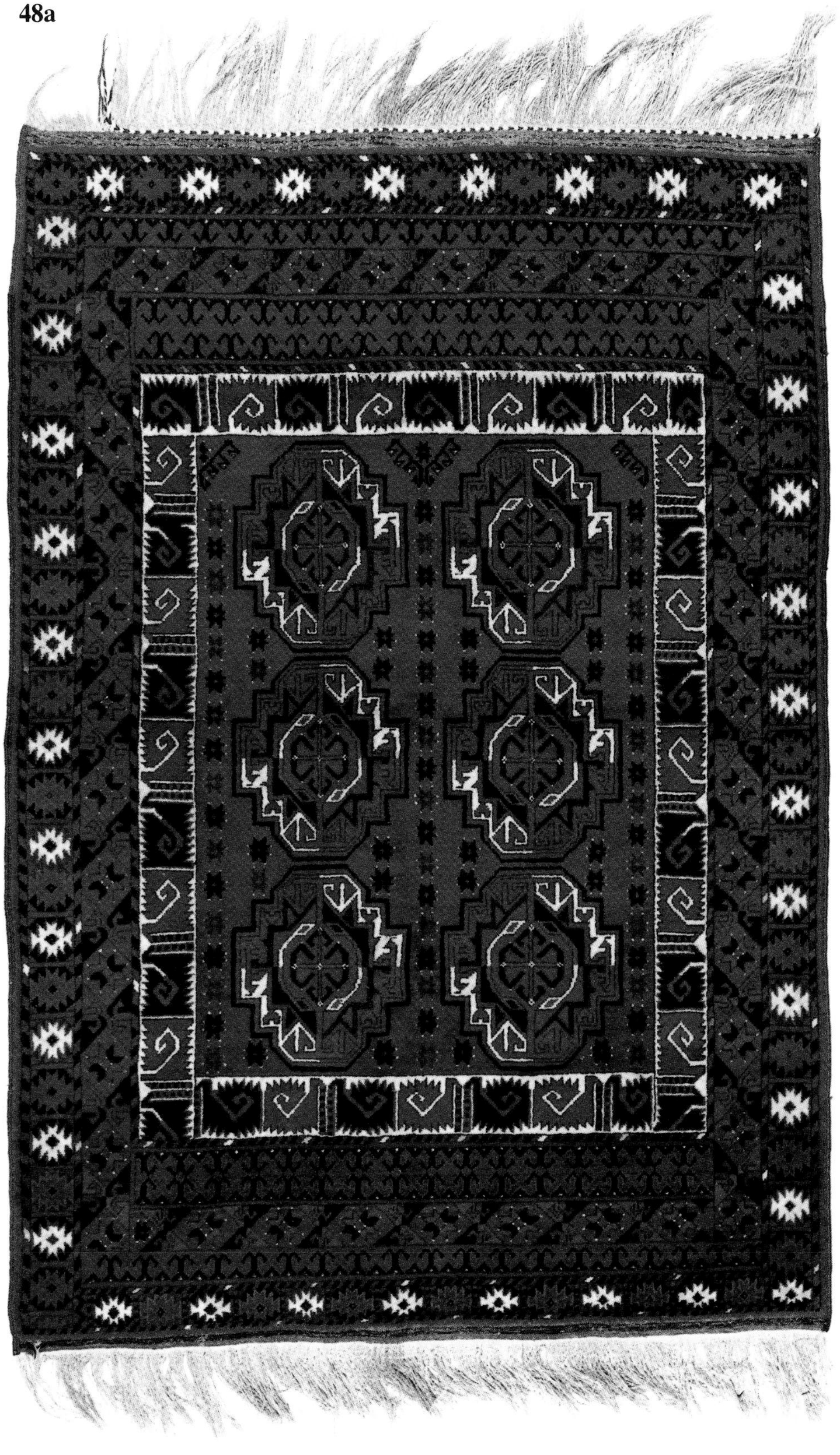

Colour Plate 48a BABA SIDIQ.
*This rug, with an entirely
typical construction, handle and
weave, depicts a design which
overall, is far from classical. A
good example of the variety and
non-conformity of classical
origins which depart from the
norm. All the individual motifs
are typical of the district —
even the large stylised Chobash
gul which somewhat resembles
the* Akhel *gul, and especially
the inner border which is
frequently seen in Baba Sidiq
production. Note that this piece
from the Qala-i-Zal district does
not have the classical kilim.
(188 x 132cm).*

Shir Khosrow Paiwand

present two hundred, all inhabited by Tekke Turkomans. They abandoned the last of their *yurts* around 1976 and now live in mud-brick dwellings set in compounds. From the day of their arrival in the early 1930s, they began making carpets, as they always have done, in order to augment their income, and despite this commercialisation of their traditional craft, they did not lower their standards of craftsmanship or materials.

Although their ancient homeland tradition was to weave single-wefted pieces, the Tekkes of Barmazid, like those of Sharkh, now weave double-wefted goods. In the early years, they used only the traditional madder, but around 1943, they began to use synthetic dyestuffs as well.

In Barmazid, as well as Sharkh, the weavers use a technique which is unique in Afghanistan. Immediately after the woollen weft is passed through the warps, a thick damp 'false' cotton weft is followed. This 'buffer' cotton weft is beaten down with great vigour, ensuring that the thin single-ply woollen weft remains undamaged. When this woollen weft is beaten tightly enough, the cotton weft is extracted, to be reused.

The Barmazid Tekkes have remained faithful to their age-old rendering of the Tekke *gul,* and, as would be expected, their carpets vary little from those of the Sharkh Tekkes. There are occasional variations in the border guards, the Barmazids often having a guard composed of the *parsi* motif. Recently a few *purdahs* started to appear and these are still being produced. (See Colour Plate 46).

Among the other tribes living around the village of Barmazid, the Hazaras have learned to weave and have been copying the Tekke designs; these goods are also sold under the name of Barmazids (see page 79). These pseudo-Barmazids are of inferior quality and nearly always contain an upper weft of cotton, which though concealed by the lower woollen weft, gives the fabric an entirely different handle. The weave is regular, but because of the wefts, the individual knots are more easily distinguishable, thus making the ridges less conspicuous. Other Turkomans around Mazar also weave this Barmazid design, which makes the Barmazid production appear quite considerable. The authentic Barmazids, however, number only about four hundred pieces a year.

Barmazid Characteristics:

General:	Firm, supple handle. Clean ridged back of regular weave; tight knotting, double wefted. Synthetic and natural dyes.
Designs:	Small octagonal Tekke *gul,* some *purdahs.* All Karaqul wool; white motifs of Kandahari wool. Plain white *kilim.*
Warps:	2-ply Karaqul wool, undyed; recent introduction of imported 3-ply machine-spun yarn.
Wefts:	1-ply Karaqul wool, dyed red.
Selvedges:	Usually indigo — very neat and tight so often not visible from the top. Blanket stitch.
Knots:	Asymmetric.
Sizes:	Carpets of 6m^2 to 12m^2.

Daulatabad (Balkh)

Daulatabad (Balkh) — not to be confused with Daulatabad (Faryab) (see page 122) — produces the most carpets of the Mazar district. Apart from the carpets woven by Tekke Turkomans in Barmazid (see page 78) the main production is of pseudo-Barmazids woven by Hazaras, forcibly settled here from the Central Hazarajat, by Ersaris and by a few Uzbeks in villages around Daulatabad. They have learned both the craft and the design from the Tekkes. With a few exceptions, even the best of these goods, which vary considerably in quality, are never as fine as the genuine Tekke Barmazid, although they are sold under that name. Despite an overall similarity, the difference in weave is noticeable on the back of the carpet, being less regular and often with less distinct ridges. Prices of these goods average some fifty per cent less than for corresponding qualities in the genuine Tekke production.

Daulatabad (Balkh) Characteristics:

General:	Firm, fairly supple handle. Ridged back; tightness of weave according to quality. Double wefted. Synthetic dyes. Design: small Tekke *gul*. All Karaqul wool; Kandahari wool for white motifs. Plain off-white *kilim*.
Colours:	Red, indigo, white.
Warps:	2-ply undyed Karaqul wool.
Wefts:	2-ply Karaqul wool dyed red; often one cotton weft dyed red concealed by a second woollen weft.
Selvedges:	Red, blue or natural undyed dark wool; blanket stitch.
Knots:	Asymmetric.
Sizes:	All sizes: 1.5m² to 12m², mostly 6m² (170 x 90 to 400 x 300 mostly 300 x 200cm).

For the sake of clarity, the other areas which constitute the Mazar production are classed into groups which make carpets and rugs of similar quality.

Keldar and Baba Sidiq

These two centres produce carpets and rugs first in the order of quality and fineness. Keldar (actually in Samangan Province) produces mainly *purdahs*, which have been described in Chapter 4.

Baba Sidiq is a small village of some two hundred houses, about seventy-five kilometres north-east of Mazar, and named after a shrine at the outskirts of the village. Baba Sidiq goods are fine and well made. The most frequent design is the *alma gul* on a variety of fields, with the typical Beshiri border always present. (See Colour Plate 48).

Baba Sidiq is near the best carpet-producing villages of the Qala-i-Zal *woleswali* near Kunduz, and not surprisingly, this has had a beneficial influence on both the design and the construction of the Baba Sidiq goods.

Baba Sidiq Characteristics:

General:	Firm, supple handle. Finely ridged back; tight knotting. Double wefted. Synthetic dyes.
Designs:	Mainly *alma gul,* some others. All Karaqul wool; Kandahari wool for white motifs. Usually plain off-white *kilim*.
Colours:	Various reds; orange gold, indigo green, white.
Warps:	2-ply undyed Karaqul wool.

Colour Plate 49 A section of an ISLAM carpet. This border motif is very typical of the Islam production which almost invariably comprises large and oversize carpets. Both primary and secondary guls *are those of the current Taghan production. (329 x 265cm).*

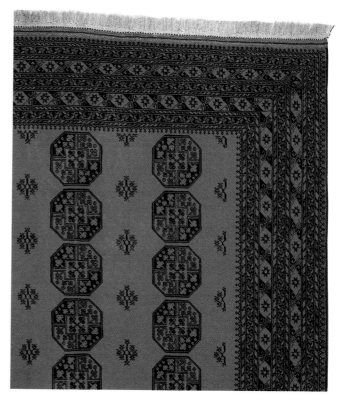

49

Colour Plate 50 QAZAN carpet. The main distinguishing feature of the Qazans is the dotted band around the primary gul, *and the invariable use of the 'eight flower' motif as the secondary gul. It is probably the Qazan gul which is so often referred to in books as the Ersari gul-i-gul. (256 x 171cm).*

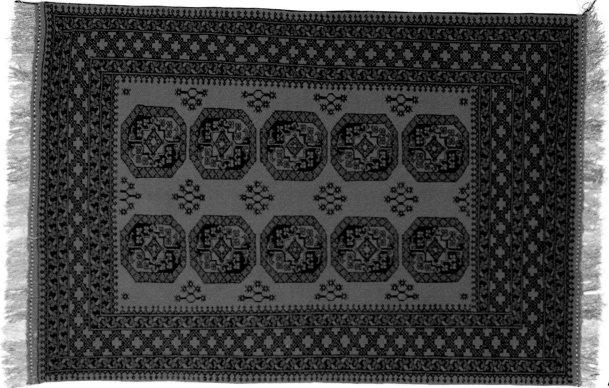

50

51

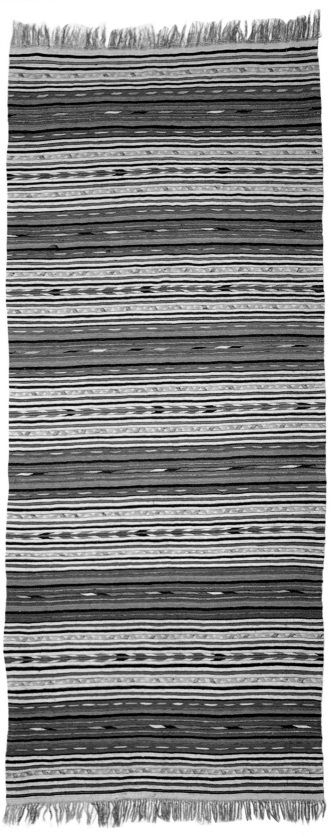

Colour Plate 51 A DALI KILIM. *The older pieces are considerably finer than contemporary production which also tend to be redder and contain cruder colours. The Turkomans call this fabric, which is generally long and narrow,* ghajari *a term used by them for all lightweight tapestry weaves. (280 x 121cm).*

52

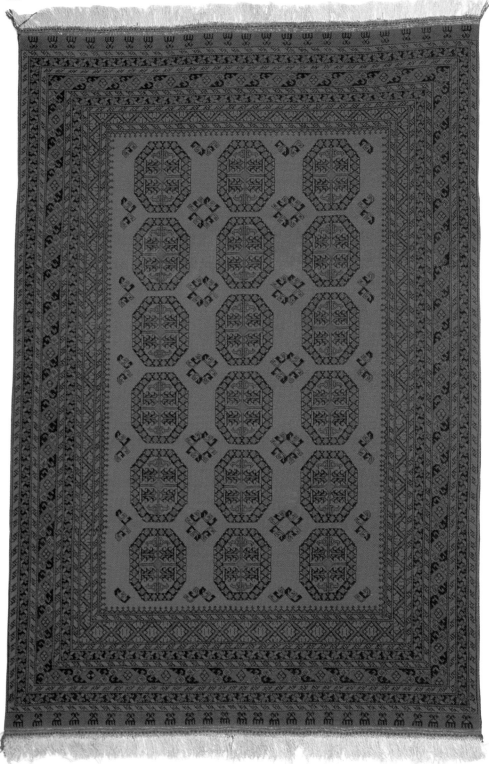

Colour Plate 52 *A DALI carpet. The three main design characteristics of the Dali production are: (i) The 'comb' motif almost invariably appears at both ends of the piece. (ii) The primary gul, as in the Qazan, is encircled by a band studded with small rectilinear motifs. (iii) the 'Christmas Tree' or inverted ribcage' motif appears in at least two quadrants of each main gul.*

In the piece illustrated, it appears in all four quadrants. This motif is also found in the older Sulayman rugs from the Kunduz area as well as in practically all older Qarqeen carpets. (296 x 205cm).

53

Colour Plate 53 An UZBEK embroidered NAMAD typical of the Khairabad production. (198 x 97cm).
Courtesy Josephine Powell

Wefts:	2-ply undyed Karaqul wool; use of cotton wefts rare.
Knots:	Asymmetric.
Selvedges:	Indigo, blanket stitch.
Sizes:	2.5m² to 5m²
	(200 x 150cm to 280 x 180cm).

Islam, Chobash, Dali, Hairaton, Aruq Bador

These villages are on or near the Amu Darya (Oxus) River and their production is next in order of quality, which is good to average. Traditionally, the wool used in carpets from Islam is particularly well sorted and carded. This can be appreciated in the brilliant sheen which develops after a relatively short period of use. The Islam carpet has also a distinctive border motif (see Colour Plate 49). An unusual number of oversize carpets up to 20m² are produced here, and these being woven out of doors are mainly marketed in the autumn.

The Mazar Chobash carpet, not to be confused with the Sheberghan Chobash, is easily recognised by its unique *fil-pai gul,* with alternate quadrants of white and sometimes with some green in the borders.

The carpets from Dali and Hairaton today generally display the Dali and Qazan *fil-pai* respectively; and the carpets from Aruq Bador, the Bokhara *gul,* often known as *kar-i-sefide* (white work). (See Colour Plates 50, 51 and 52).

Characteristics:

General:	Supple handle. Slightly ridged back; tight knotting. Double wefted. Synthetic dyes; natural dyes rare.
Designs:	Islam: *fil-pai;* Dali: *fil-pai;* Hairaton: the Qazan *fil-pai;* Aruq Bador: Bokhara *gul.* All Karaqul wool; Kandahari wool for white motifs. Plain red *kilim.*
Colours:	Red, indigo, white rare, except for Bokhara *gul* in Aruq Bador production; and in Chobash *fil-pai,* which may contain green.
Warps:	2-ply undyed Karaqul wool.
Wefts:	2-ply undyed Karaqul wool.
Selvedges:	Red, indigo, blanket stitch.
Knots:	Asymmetric.
Sizes:	Islam: up to 20m², others 6m² to 8-9m².

Shor Tepe, Shor Aruq, Taj Goza

These three centres, north of Mazar on the Amu Darya River, produce rugs that can be characterised by coarse yarn and poor quality workmanship. Designs are varied. In Shor Tepe, the Bokhara *gul* is predominant; in Shor Aruq and Taj Goza, the Bokhara, *fil-pai* and *alma gul* all appear. Cotton is invariably used in at least one weft in this production.

Characteristics:

General:	Hard or spongy handle. Slightly ridged back; loose knotting. Double wefted. Synthetic dyestuffs.
Designs:	Shor Tepe: Bokhara *gul;* Shor Aruq and Taj Goza: Bokhara

54

Colour Plate 54 *CHARCHANGI mat from Aq Chah. Whilst the centre of this piece is absolutely typical, the border guards would be different in larger pieces. The use of orange in primary guls of the traditional Aq Chah production is rare. The Aq Chah Charchangi is a notable exception. (69 x 52cm).*

gul, fil-pai, and *alma gul.* All Karaqul wool; cotton weft; Kandahari wool for white motifs. Plain red *kilim.*

Colours: Red, indigo, light blue, black, orange, green, white.
Warps: 2-ply undyed Karaqul wool.
Wefts: 2-ply Karaqul dyed red wool; sometimes one or both wefts of cotton dyed red.
Selvedges: Red, indigo; blanket stitch.
Knots: Asymmetric.
Sizes: 2.5m² and 2 x 1m; few carpet sizes (200 x 125 and 200 x 100cm).

Kawk and Khamyab

Production from these two villages is only a little better than that of the Qarqeens (see page 70), that is to say, of very low quality. These coarse, cheap and unattractive pieces are made with poor yarn dyed with the cheapest synthetic dyes, and always have at least one cotton weft. The use of hemp is not unknown. Designs range from the *fil-pai* to variations of the Bokhara or *alma gul.*

Characteristics:

General: Spongy handle; dry feel. Coarse ridged back; loose knotting. Double wefted. Synthetic dyes.
Designs: *Fil-pai,* Bokhara *gul,* and *alma gul.* Poor quality (dead) Karaqul wool; Kandahari wool for white motifs. Plain red *kilim.*
Colours: Red, indigo, light blue, black, orange, white.
Warps: 2- or 3-ply undyed Karaqul wool.
Wefts: 2-ply undyed Karaqul wool; upper weft of cotton sometimes dyed red.
Selvedges: Red, black, indigo or blue, undyed black; blanket stitch.
Knots: Asymmetric.
Sizes: Carpets 6m², rugs 2 x 1m (300 x 200cm).

Khairabad

Khairabad, some forty kilometres west of Mazar, is inhabited mainly by Uzbeks, and although some of them began making rugs around 1975, the production is insignificant. The usual motif of these coarse rugs is the *kar-i-sefide,* a Bokhara-type *gul.*

Uzbeks from these regions formerly wove *kilims,* which can still be found in some markets of Afghanistan. The Khairabad *kilim* was woven in narrow, twenty-five centimetre bands and then sewn together. The 'floating weft' technique was used, that is, the weft of individual colour skipping warps in order to make the design. Various geometric central Asian motifs were used in each band and the whole formed a most colourful and harmonious ensemble.

Today, Khairabad is the main centre for those gaudily embroidered felt rugs called *namads.* A design in the most vivid colours is embroidered in cotton or artificial silk on the black background of the *namad,* and the edge is sewn with a twisted cord of various colours. The quality of these *namads* varies considerably, from a thin and floppy texture to a thick and firm one. (See Colour Plate 53).

Chapter 7
The Aq Chah Production

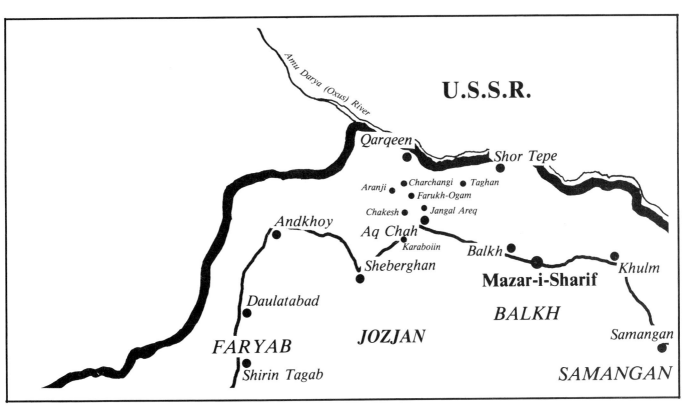

Aq Chah is the main administrative centre for over one hundred villages scattered across the plain of Afghan Turkestan. It is some ninety kilometres west of Mazar, from which it can be reached in little over an hour along the paved road forming part of the northern Circular Route. Aq Chah has the largest and most important carpet bazaar in Afghanistan. From here between 150,000m²-200,000m² of carpets and rugs are marketed annually. Every major exporter has either a manager or representative posted here, who attends the bi-weekly bazaar (see page 60). At night, the intermittent cries of the *chowkidars,* the night watchmen paid by the municipality, echo through the streets of Aq Chah reassuring each other that all is safe from both two and four-legged marauders, for even today, armed bands of brigands waylay the late traveller and leave him stripped of clothes and possessions.

Although there have been Turkomans settled in the region of Aq Chah for over one hundred and fifty years, the majority came across the Amu Darya (Oxus) River in the early 1920s to settle in this northern region of Afghanistan.

Generally speaking, this is an arid, sandy and flat region, subject to frequent and severe sandstorms. Water from even the deepest wells is often brackish, though not as much as in Andkhoy to the north-west. Cotton, corn and maize are grown in the irrigated areas as well as melons and grapes. A splash of orange on the flat mud roof signifies that maize cobs are being sun dried for

A section of the Aq Chah bazaar

Colour Plate 55 FARUKH-OGAM *carpet. (236 x 172cm).*

Colour Plate 56 FARUKH-QALA. *As the photograph shows, the main difference is in the border composition. A distinguishing feature of the Farukh production is that the trefoil motif in the primary* gul *is oval, sometimes almost pointed, and is reminiscent of an acorn in its cup. The Farukh secondary* gul *is invariably a thinner, but more detailed version of the 'stepped pyramid' motif which is used by the Sulaymans of Andkhoy and Aq Chah as well as in the production from both Alti Bolaq and Daulatabad. (188 x 149cm).*

Colour Plate 57 Semi-antique JANGAL AREQ *prayer rug. The important distiguishing feature of this piece is the main border guard, which is typical of much of the older production from this large village. An unusual feature of this piece is that the wefts are dyed red. By and large, the Jangal Areq production has deteriorated in quality over recent years. (137 x 89cm).*

Colour Plate 58 A JANGAL AREQ *rug. This is a very typical example of the smaller sizes which are now made in this centre. (148 x 72cm).*

57

58

59   **60**

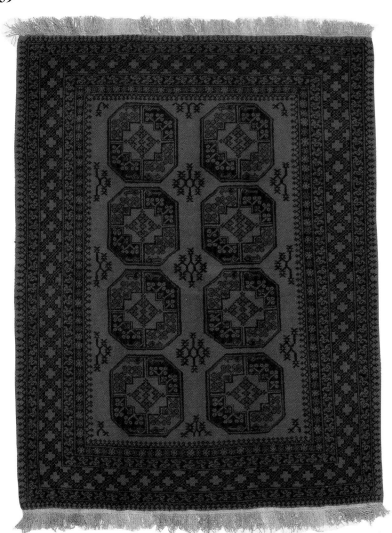

Colour Plate 59 A small CHAKESH carpet. The true Chakesh, easily recognised by the dotted diamond-shaped motif in the centre of the fil-pai gul, *is one of the best and most durable qualities in Aq Chah.the seconday* gul *is invariably the 'eight flower' motif, in whole or in part. (225 x 177cm).*

Colour Plate 60 Another example of a Chakesh design. This design is very similar to the dyrnak gul *which is so closely associated with the* Yamouds. Another example of the way in which Turkoman motifs are found to be common to various tribes, clans and sub-clans. (140 x 70cm).

A serai in Aq Chah on market day

A Turkoman carpet dealer in a serai

winter use. Sesame seeds are also grown here. A blindfolded camel harnessed to a wooden crusher ceaselessly treads his way around and around a vat of sesame seed, extracting the edible oil so highly prized in local Turkoman cooking. Mulberry trees provide fruit, which is dried and stored, and leaves for the silkworms. The exportation of silk cocoons to Japan is a minor secondary industry. Karaqul pelts, destined for the London and Leningrad auction houses, is also an important industry. However, irrigated and fertile soil is scarce, and many villages around Aq Chah depend on a livelihood from carpet making, which indeed is the major local industry.

The hundred villages or so around Aq Chah are inhabited primarily by Turkomans, practically all of Ersari stock. There are some Uzbeks, Pashtuns and Arabis, and although these tribes do not weave carpets, they are not entirely removed from the industry, for some are flock masters and others are engaged in ancillary trades such as spinning and dyeing.

The bulk of the carpet production comes from fourteen villages, many of which, confusingly, bear names, often of clans, common to Turkoman villages in other parts of Afghan Turkestan, for instance, Dali, Islam, Qazan, which exist also in the Mazar area, and Chobash which is a major centre near Sheberghan and also in the Mazar region. Besides this confusion, the increasing intermarriage among Ersari clans and the trend towards abandoning characteristic clan designs in favour of what is fashionable at the moment, makes it more and more difficult to pinpoint any specific place of origin of a carpet from this area.

For example, from 1975 to 1978, about seventy per cent of the Aq Chah production was the *kar-i-sefide* (white work), that is, small Bokhara-type *guls* and secondary motifs in white. Twenty per cent was *kar-i-surkh* (red work) or the elephant foot design, and ten per cent various other designs.

Less than a year later, *kar-i-sefide* made up only fifty per cent of the production, and the *kar-i-surkh* had risen to forty per cent.

Previously, both wefts were of undyed wool, whereas now wefts are frequently dyed red. Another example of the continual change taking place in the Afghan carpet industry was the introduction of cotton wefts in 1971/2. In order to camouflage this regrettable break from tradition, the cotton wefts were dyed red. Today about half of the Aq Chah production has dyed cotton wefts.

Not a great deal is known about Afghan carpets prior to the early 1950s, for up to this period Afghanistan was a closed country. In the decade leading to the outbreak of the last war, the Western world undergoing its near catastrophic slump was not interested in Oriental carpets. Those Afghan carpets that did find their way to Europe or the United States had been exported from the Soviet Union or through Meshed in Iran. However, it does seem that a high proportion of these pieces contained natural dyestuffs, particularly indigo and madder. Likewise, most of the older pieces — many being from dowries — which were later exported from Afghanistan, also contained natural dyestuffs. The effective commercialisation of Afghan carpets dates from the war and gave rise to the widespread use of chemical dyes.

Apart from the use of cotton wefts, the overall standard of the Aq Chah production seems to have improved in the last six or seven years. Roughly ten per cent of the Aq Chah goods are in the good to well above average range, with only about thirty per cent falling into the poor category. Many of these latter pieces are exported to the Jeddah market in Saudi Arabia.

Tent furnishings such as *boleshts, juwals,* and *khourjeens* are also made in the Aq Chah region by diverse clans.

In Aq Chah, all sizes of carpets and rugs are produced, ranging from 12m² (400 x 300cm) to mats of 0.35m² (75 x 45cm). The small pieces are often made by children and are their first 'teeth cutting' exercises.

Of the fourteen principal carpet producing villages, seven are worthy of special attention.

Charchangi (literally the four corners, or four angles)

This village lies about twenty-five kilometres north of Aq Chah and derived its name from the Charchangi clan of Ersari Turkomans which settled there in the early 1920s. They are of the same clan as the Charchangis of Andkhoy, but since their arrival in Aq Chah they have been weaving a completely different design from those of Andkhoy. Thus, when referring to a Charchangi carpet, one must specify Aq Chah or Andkhoy. There are Charchangis in other parts of Afghan Turkestan, notably in Daulatabad (Faryab) but they weave yet a different carpet. (See page 115).

Like so many other clans in Aq Chah the Charchangis appear to have abandoned their former design (see Colour Plate 54) in favour of the *kar-i-sefide*.

A caravan heading for the Aq Chah bazaar

Farukh

There are two main villages which have taken their names from the Farukh clan who live therein. Farukh Qala is some fifteen kilometres to the north-east of Aq Chah, whilst Farukh-Ogam lies some fifteen kilometres to the west of Aq Chah.

Farukh-Ogam has been inhabited by members of the Ogam and Farukh clans for over one hundred and fifty years. Unaffected by the upheavels suffered by so many Turkomans obliged to flee from their homeland in the southern part of Russia, these two clans have, to a greater extent, been able to maintain their traditional way of life. The elders to the village still remember their semi-nomadic days when every spring they moved their belongings, *yurts* and flocks to farther pasture land. Today they live in mud-brick houses yet some still keep their *yurts* in their compounds to be used as day-rooms by the women and children. Traditionally, the Ogam and Farukhs wove rugs 2m² to 2.5m² (200 x 100 and 200 x 125cm), but it is for their large and oversize carpets, still being made today, that they are famed. (A Farukh carpet measuring approximately 97m² is today in one of the main banks of Kabul. This carpet was made about fifty years ago by fourteen weavers on a specially constructed loom.

The Farukhs were among the last Turkomans in Aq Chah to use *kermes,* and when this dyestuff became too rare and costly, they substituted a bluey-pink synthetic dye to simulate the *kermes* red, but generally speaking, this, too, was abandoned around 1973, when they took up the same reds as seen in the overall Aq Chah production.

Although there are both Ogams and Farukhs in the Sheberghan area and in Daulatabad, the main Farukh production comes from Aq Chah. (See Colour Plates 55 and 56).

Jangal Areq (meaning the woods of Areq, the English word 'jungle' comes from *jangal*)

This large village on the old dirt road from Mazar and twenty kilometres east of Aq Chah comprises some three thousand houses, and is inhabited by various Ersari clans. Jangal Areq has given its name to a design rather than to

61

62

Colour Plate 61 A zir-i-pai *ARANJI rug, literally 'underfoot' or used piece. The gul is the hallmark of the Aranji clan. Note the white motif called* barmak, *which means finger/ fingernail and is much favoured in the Labijar production. (189 x 110cm).*

Colour Plate 62 TAGHAN BALAH. The truer and more traditional Taghan gul is that shown under Taghan Labijar (see Colour Plate 68). Recent production contains many variations. The secondary gul is nearly always a form of the 'eight flower' motif, though the 'stepped pyramid' is occasionally seen. (191 x 155cm).

63

Colour Plate 63 A semi-antique KARABOIIN KHOURJEEN. (120 x 60cm).

61a

63a

Colour Plate 61a ARANJI. This well-preserved piece dates from circa 1950. In the field of madder mixed with walnut are the two rows of classical Aranji guls. The intricate border, featuring six guards on either side of a typical Labijar border motif in white, suggests a strong Sheberghan-Labijar influence. The weave, however, is typical Aranji, and one wonders whether the execution of this piece was influenced by intermarriage between two Ersari-Turkoman clans. (204 x 110cm).

Shir Khosrow Paiwand

Colour Plate 63a A fairly classical KARABOIIN rug dating from circa 1930. Knotted in the Aq Chan district, this piece is noteworthy for both the intricate border and a field of kermes *(cochineal). The selvedges are goat hair. The disparity in design between the top and bottom centre guards (main border) is indicative of the fact that Turkoman rugs are made from memory. (228 x 133cm).*

Shir Khosrow Paiwand

A section of a typical Jangal Areq rug, of commercial quality

a clan motif. The Jangal Areq primary *gul* is small and squarish; the secondary *gul* is reminiscent of the secondary *gul* of the classic Tekke carpet (see page 78) and is loosely called the Bokhara design or *kar-i-sefide*.

In 1979 the only 'carpet factory' still functioning in Afghanistan was at Jangal Areq. It is owned by a large exporter and serves him a useful function, both for publicity purposes as well as a source of supply. Local youths weave carpets in two large buildings, using wool dyed on the premises and producing designs and colour combinations which are, in the main, not traditional. It is said that the introduction of cotton wefts began here, the reason being that this exporter was pressed by his foreign connections into doing so. This unfortunate habit later spread to other areas. (See Colour Plates 57 and 58).

Chakesh

This is another large village, north of Aq Chah, mainly inhabited by members of the Chakesh (Ersari) clan. Some of the best carpets of the Aq Chah region come from here and from the village of Sharbak, some five kilometres to the north-east of Aq Chah. They are easily identified by the diamond-shaped motif in the centre of the *fil-pai gul*. However, one must differentiate between the pseudo-Chakesh, that is the same design woven by other tribes in the Aq Chah area. The genuine Chakesh carpet has a particularly tight and regular weave and is especially dense, yet supple. (See Colour Plate 59).

The Chakesh clan also weaves another design containing white which is a coarse rendering of the classical Russian Yamoud *dyrnak gul*. (See Colour Plate 60).

Although there are Chakesh living in Andkhoy, another major carpet-making district, they have not woven their traditional motifs since the early 1970s. These earlier Andkhoy-Chakesh pieces can be recognised by an orange-red colour, dyed red wefts, and a border motif of the rosettes in indigo and black associated with Andkhoy goods.

Aranji

A small village of that name is situated some twelve kilometres to the north-west of Aq Chah. Largely inhabited by Turkomans of the Aranji sub-clan, this used to be the main source of rugs bearing this distinctive clan *gul*.

As with most other Turkomans, members of the Aranji sub-clan are found throughout the Aq Chah region, but in those villages where they find themselves in a small minority, they have tended to abandon their traditional design for those made by the local majority. (See Colour Plate 61).

Taghan (Balah)

A large village to the east of Aq Chah and situated slightly to the north of the old road to Mazar. Production from this village and its satellite hamlets is considerable, but there are Taghans throughout the area. This, no doubt, is one reason for the variance in the modern production. (See Colour Plate 62).

Karaboiin

A smallish, very elongated village some seven kilometres to the south of Aq Chah town, in which *yurts* can still be seen dotted about amongst the more prevalent mud dwellings in which the majority of Turkomans now live.

Alas, the Karaboiins have almost abandoned their traditional designs over the last few years. A feature of the older Karaboiin production is that the vast majority of those pieces which are to be found today have oxidised into lovely shades of rich browns. (See Colour Plate 63).

Characteristics of Aq Chah Production:

In such a large and varied production, it is not possible to give specific characteristics; however, the following general remarks can be applied to most of the Aq Chah production:

General: Handle various, from firm for better quality pieces to floppy and spongy for poor quality. Some pieces have a 'plywood' back caused by too thick cotton being used in the wefts, and a thin pile. Variable ridged back, tightness of knotting according to quality. Double wefted. Synthetic dyestuffs throughout.

Designs: Mainly *kar-i-sefide, fil-pai,* some others. Mainly Karaqul wool for pile; warps of Karaqul or Ghilzai wool; Kandahari wool for white motifs. Mostly red *kilims,* some with designs.

Colours: Red, indigo, black, also orange, gold, occasionally green, white.

Warps: 2- or sometimes 3-ply undyed Karaqul or Ghilzai wool.

Wefts: 2-ply undyed or red Karaqul wool; ninety per cent of production with one cotton weft.

Selvedges: Red, blue or undyed; sometimes goat hair; blanket stitch.

Knots: Asymmetric.

Sizes: 0.35m^2 to 12m^2, including runners 75cm x 45cm to 400cm to 300cm.

96

64

Colour Plate 64 A semi-antique KIZILAYAK. Whilst the design is very typical, the squarish shape is not. This piece is one of a pair bought in Cairo by the author. (106 x 88cm).
Author's collection

67

Colour Plate 67 A semi-antique KIZILAYAK prayer rug. The border is very typical of much of the Kizilayak production. (117 x 79cm).

65

66

Colour Plate 65. This oldish KIZILAYAK prayer rug is not a very common design. The duck-egg blue in the cross and inner guard is a shade which appears in many of the older Taghans from Sheberghan. (96 x 67cm).
Author's collection

Colour Plate 66 Section of a KIZILAYAK runner. The primary gul in this piece is typical of its origin, and is very similar to the secondary gul in the Saruq production. (293 x 75cm).

67a

Colour Plate 67a An old and ornate KIZILAYAK prayer rug. Knotted with hand-spun yarn dyed with natural dyestuffs, this piece dates from the turn of the century. It is of interest for two reasons: firstly, the classical and main Kizilayak border is absent, having been replaced by the badam *(almond) motif and, secondly, the complex design now appears in a limited Beluch-type production from a small area to the southwest of Herat. However, in this Beluch production fugitive dyes are used, which detracts greatly from an otherwise innovative and evolutionary trend. It is not known exactly when or how and why this change occurred. (152 x 88cm).*

Shir Khosrow Paiwand

Chapter 8
The Sheberghan Production

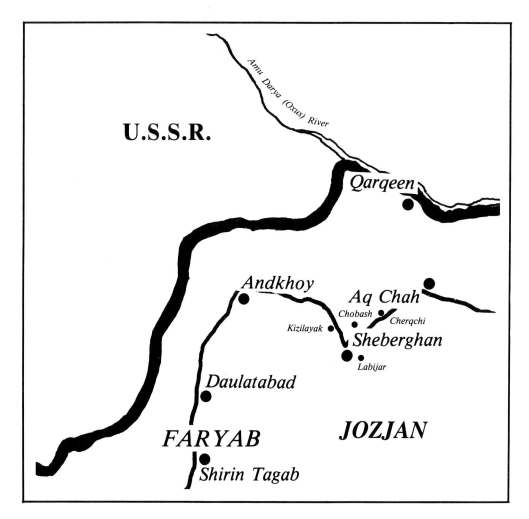

Sheberghan, the capital of Jozjan Province, is a prosperous town largely populated by Uzbeks, which at the turn of the century was the seat of an independent Khanate. It lies at the end of the tarred section of the north Circular Route and its importance today is mainly due to the nearby natural gas fields discovered in 1960. Much of this natural gas is piped to the Soviet Union whose frontier is some two hundred kilometres to the north. This industry provides employment and consequently, trade. Both of these factors have had an adverse effect on the local carpet industry, and the Sheberghan is no longer the important carpet-marketing centre which it was up to the mid-1960s. In fact, in 1978, Sheberghan boasted only one carpet shop and a few others selling *kilims* which came mostly from Sari-Pul.

The current Sheberghan production is approximately 60,000 m² annually, of which half comes from Kizilayak and its environs. The individuality and overall quality of the Sheberghan production as a whole has sadly deteriorated. No longer does one see the lovely colour combinations resulting from the use of natural dyestuffs which was one of the distinguishing features of the older carpets made in this area. Neither does one find in the current production the Labijar design or the characteristic Saltuq carpet with the Tree of Life motif running along the outside of the two exterior rows of *guls*.

The use of natural dyestuffs, furthermore, has completely given way to synthetic ones. One, sometimes both wefts, are of cotton. Except for the Sheberghan Chobash carpets, most of the traditional designs of the area have been simplified and adulterated to such an extent that they have entirely lost their individual characteristics. Thus, it is virtually impossible to ascertain their clan origins with any precision. A considerable proportion of the pieces made in the Sheberghan area are now sold in the Aq Chah bazaar, where they have become as raspberries in raspberry jam; a sad example of change for the worse in Afghan Turkoman carpets.

Broadly speaking, the Sheberghan carpet-producing region is not very extensive and comprises two main clusters of villages, namely Kizilayak and Labijar.

Typical Kizilayak border motifs

Kizilayak (Sheberghan)

Kizilayak, literally meaning 'red foot', is the name both of an Ersari sub-clan and of a place.

Kizilayak, with its surrounding villages, is a small town some forty-five minutes drive north from Sheberghan. The Kizilayak production, more than half the total of the Sheberghan area, is sold in its weekly Friday bazaar, often attended by dealers and exporters' agents from Aq Chah.

The Kizilayak clan has its own traditional designs and border motifs but, like the Turkomans of Andkhoy, the Kizilayaks are great copiers and adapt very quickly to fashion trends and market conditions. This means that today it is not possible to recognise the Kizilayak production by its designs alone. Furthermore, it is customary in Afghanistan to attribute to the Kizilayaks any rug of unknown origin which has a non-traditional design.

The older Kizilayak pieces, apart from their traditional designs, are identifiable by their typical weave featuring a flattish back showing fine and regular knotting, with loose wefts of very even hand-spun undyed Karaqul wool. Today's Kizilayak production, almost entirely in small and medium rug sizes, is varied in both quality and designs, which are mainly *kar-i-sefide*. Only about ten per cent of the total production can be said to be slightly above average Aq Chah quality; at least thirty per cent is poor. Much of this inferior production is exported to Jeddah in Saudi Arabia. (See Colour Plates 64, 65, 66 and 67).

Kizilayak Characteristics:

General: Floppy, spongy, stiff or firm handle, according to quality. Weave and general appearance of the back variable according to quality; coarse knotting, double wefted, synthetic dyes.

Designs: Numerous and variable. Karaqul wool used but an increasing tendency to use Kandahari and Ghilzai wool, especially for white motifs.

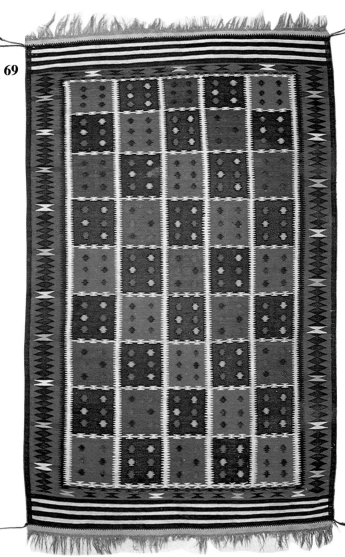

Colour Plate 68 A semi-antique TAGHAN prayer rug from the village of Taghan-Labijar. This is a very typical interpretation of the Taghan primary gul. The current Taghan production is very varied, and generally the fil-pai gul is larger than portrayed here. (83 x 57cm).

Colour Plate 69 A very typical LABIJAR KILIM. These fine pieces, nearly always with a panel design, are generally much larger than this one, and are to be found in sizes of over twenty metres. The construction is invariably tapestry weave. (325 x 208cm).

Colour Plate 70 Oldish WAZIRI rug woven in Andkhoy with natural dyestuffs. (122 x 73cm).

Author's collection

71

72

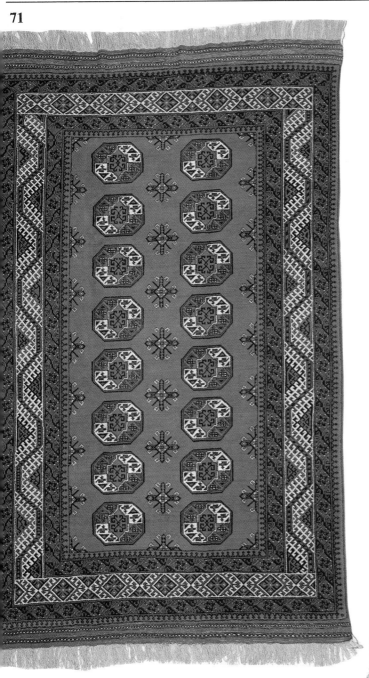

Colour Plate 71 CHOBASH carpet. In spite of variations in the primary and secondary guls, the Chobash is very easily differentiated from all other Ersari 'elephant's foot' guls because it is the only one in which the alternate quadrants are white. Most Chobashes come from the Sheberghan area, but members of this clan are also numerous in both the Kunduz and Mazar regions, where differences are to be seen in the border designs which sometimes contain some motifs in green. (306 x 198cm).

Colour Plate 72 A good quality CHERQCHI rug. The very small primary gul, which is a typical and distinguishing feature of this production, is often referred to as the 'cat's foot'. The stylised rosette in the secondary guard is typical of the Sheberghan production. (190 x 101cm).

Part of a rug measuring 132 x 72cm. The primary gul is an octohedron divided into its eight segments — one of the older Sulayman motifs. The inner border guard features the 'broken rectangle' or a triangle with a stepped hypotenuse — a motif favoured by the Kizilayaks and which only appears in the production from the area. Thus, this piece is a Sulayman design woven in the Kizilayak region.

Colours:	Red, blue, indigo, red or white *kilims,* gold, orange, aubergine.
Warps:	2-or 3-ply Karaqul undyed wool; also Ghilzai wool.
Wefts:	2-ply Karaqul wool, dyed red; and red cotton weft.
Selvedges:	Red, royal blue, indigo or undyed wool; blanket stitch.
Knots:	Asymmetric.
Sizes:	Small sizes from 0.6m² to 3m², some 6m² carpets. 90cm x 60cm to 200cm x 150cm.

Labijar

Labijar, meaning 'on the edge of the canal', is an area comprising four large adjoining villages situated near the Darya Safide River. Labijar, a very old settlement, is inhabited by Ersari Turkomans of whom the majority belong to the Qara clan, also by Saltuq Turkomans, and their carpets and rugs have a reputation for being of good quality.

Although pieces from here are still well made, they are less distinctive and more standardised and could easily be mistaken for goods from Andkhoy or for the better quality carpets from Aq Chah. The older well-known Labijar designs, a spiky *gul* somewhere between that of the Saruq tribe and the Aranji Ersari sub-clan and the crenellated white border motif, are hardly ever seen in current production. Likewise, the beautiful Taghan carpets which came from the village of Taghan-Labijar, distinguishable from Taghans of other areas by their unique colour composition, have been replaced by run-of-the-mill goods which resemble many other pieces made in this area. (See Colour Plate 68).

The old Taghans from Taghan-Labijar often had dark indigo contrasting with pale indigo. In the borders, one would see bluey-green motifs highlighted by specks of gold, all on a multitoned field of madder.

A distinguishing feature of many older pieces from the Labijar area is the single or double border guard comprising small rosettes, often in a pinky madder. The small rosette in present day pieces is also a pinky red, though of synthetic dyes.

The old Labijar *kilim,* with its panels of madder, indigo and often yellow gold, each panel having a double-ended arrowhead motif in the centre, was one of the most striking of the Turkoman *kilims* (see Colour Plate 69). These large *kilims,* often from 15m² to 18m², (600cm x 300cm or even bigger) are no longer being made in Labijar, though the design is presently being copied by some Hazaras in Sari-Pul.

Today, the majority of goods from Labijar display the Alti Bolaq design, another form of *kar-i-sefide.* Synthetic dyestuffs are used and generally only medium to large rugs are made. However, a few 6m² (300cm x 200cm) carpets also come from here.

Labijar Characteristics:

Carpets from Labijar today have so lost their individuality and so closely resemble goods from Andkhoy that it is of no interest to attempt to specify contemporary characteristics.

The Waziri Design

No one really knows how or when this striking design was introduced into Afghanistan. It is sometimes ascribed to the Pashtun Waziri clan who lived in

A tribal elder from Sheberghan

the south-east of the country, but who have no carpet-making traditions whatsoever. This hypothesis is unacceptable to the author. A far more likely explanation is that this design was commissioned by a *wazir,* that is, a minister or notable resident of the Sheberghan region. This supposition is given weight by the fact that some of the very old pieces are of unusual size, including runners of extraordinary length and wider than normal, which suggests that they were made to order for a very large private house or administrative building.

The earliest pieces found in Afghanistan bearing this design are at least eighty years old, and were almost certainly made in the Sheberghan area. This opinion is based on both the weave and the colour combination. The Waziri design has now become a classic amongst Afghan Turkoman carpets. The best and most elaborately executed Waziri designs are today made in Andkhoy by various Ersari clans. A simple version in basic reds, indigo and white is produced in Kizilayak and Aq Chah again by different clans. (See Colour Plate 70).

Chobash (Sheberghan)

The Chobash, an Ersari sub-clan, have given their name to two villages, upper and lower Chobash, or Chob-Balah and Chob-Payan, both within sight of Kizilayak. Their carpets are generally of good quality.

The Chobash have, as a whole, remained faithful to their traditional designs, the best known of which is the typical Afghan *fil-pai* octagon with alternate quadrants in white. In each quadrant is a motif which has variously been described as a double-headed bird, an antelope, a dog or a fox. Occasionally, the white in the quadrant is replaced by pale red, obtained by lightly dyeing white Kandahari wool. The Sheberghan Chobash carpet has a secondary *gul* in the field and one of two distinctive border motifs which are unlike those of any other Ersari sub-clan. (See Colour Plate 71).

Cherqchi (sometimes transliterated as chiqchi)

Cherqchi is a village a few kilometres north-east of Sheberghan, just off the main road to Mazar, inhabited by the Cherqchi, an Ersari sub-clan which is known as the Chaii (literally 'from the well') in the Mazar area.

These Mazar Cherqchis are famous for their *purdahs.* However, in the Sheberghan area, the Cherqchis do not weave *purdahs,* the vast majority of their production being rugs of very average quality.

The traditional old Cherqchi design is a small squarish *gul,* locally referred to as the 'cat's paw', with no secondary motif. In the border, there was and is often seen a small rosette, a common feature in many carpets and rugs from the Sheberghan district. The size of the *gul,* while generally small, varies considerably. However, although this traditional design continues to be made, the majority of present-day Cherqchi goods have a secondary motif. (See Colour Plate 72).

Today's production, which ranges from poor quality goods using 'dead' wool to average quality often containing cotton wefts, is virtually always *kar-i-sefide,* with its red, blue and white colour combination. Most of the extremely varied modern production from Cherqchi is now sold in the Aq Chah bazaar, where it can be easily confused with goods from Jangal Areq.

71a

71b

Colour Plate 71a An old and classical CHOBASH in four panels. Of unusual size, this piece was made with hand-spun Karaqul yarn dyed with natural dyestuffs which include madder, pomegranate and sparak. (Early 20th century; 259 x 90cm).

Shir Khosrow Paiwand

Colour Plate 71b SHEBERGHAN. An interesting rug of very unusual design and size. The weave, incidence of light indigo and the madder rosettes in the border are all indicative of the origin. One wonders whether the weaver set out to make a prayer rug of unusual width, or possibly the piece may have been commissioned. (Circa 1935; 276 x 115cm).

Shir Khosrow Paiwand

73

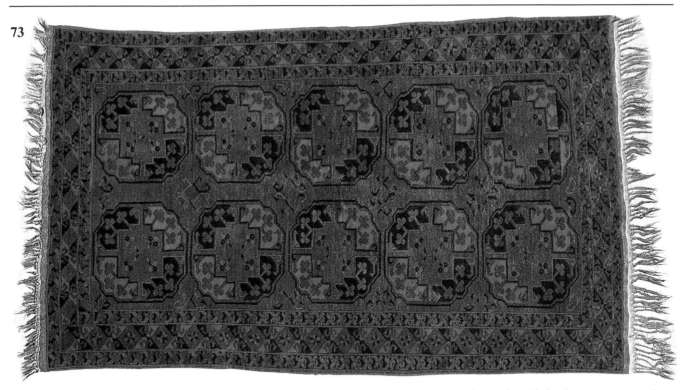

Colour Plate 73 A semi-antique SALTUQ rug. The outline shape of this gul *is very similar to the Akhel* gul, *i.e. it is somewhat smaller than the average* fil-pai, *and is indented in each quadrant. (232 x 139cm).*

75

74

Colour Plate 74 Part of a semi-antique SALTUQ carpet with the 'running dog' motif in white, which is a very typical feature of this production. This piece does not have, as a secondary gul, the elongated Tree of Life motif which is generally associated with Saltuq carpets. The main border design is very typical of the Saltuq production prior to the early '70s. (369 x 271cm).

Collection of the late W. Hayward, Esq.

Colour Plate 75 Part of a semi-antique SALTUQ carpet. Note the Tree of Life secondary motif running the whole length between the rows of primary guls, *a typical feature of this origin in pieces woven prior to 1965. The* kilim *is a good example of that found in large pieces from Labijar. (397 x 305cm).*

Saltuq 'running dog' motif

Characteristics:

There is nothing sufficiently distinctive in the Cherqchi production to merit a detailed characterisation.

The Saltuqs

Not all Saltuqs weave, and those that do are most often from *maldar* families, that is, owners of livestock. The Saltuqs from the Labijar area formerly produced carpets of superior quality with their own, unmistakable, design combinations. These were the *fil-pai* octagon of various interpretations, the elaborate secondary motifs between the vertical rows of octagons, and one or two border patterns generally framed by two narrow guards in white, having the 'running dog' motif. Sometimes the Labijar Saltuq carpet had alternating primary *guls* of totally different composition. The variety of motifs used by this comparatively small group is surprising, and these designs in all their variations are immediately recognisable as being uniquely the work of Saltuqs. (See Colour Plates 73, 74 and 75).

It is sad to relate that during the past twenty-five years, the weaving of these beautiful traditional Labijar Saltuq carpets has radically diminished. By comparison, what is produced today can be likened to a moulting, tailless peacock. The detailed and ornate primary *gul* and secondary *guls* have been replaced by an ordinary octagon and an insignificant secondary *gul*. The strong, characteristic border motifs are replaced by a number of guards of simple pattern often similar to those being woven by the Taghans of this area, and in the main only rug sizes are now being made.

The Saltuqs of Aq Chah for a long time have only woven designs which are locally fashionable. This is another example of a distinct divergence in design by members of the same tribe living in different areas.

Saltuq Characteristics:

Present-day Saltuq carpets from Labijar have retained none of their characteristics, and those of the Aq Chah Saltuqs are indistinguishable from the general Aq Chah production.

Chapter 9
The Andkhoy Production

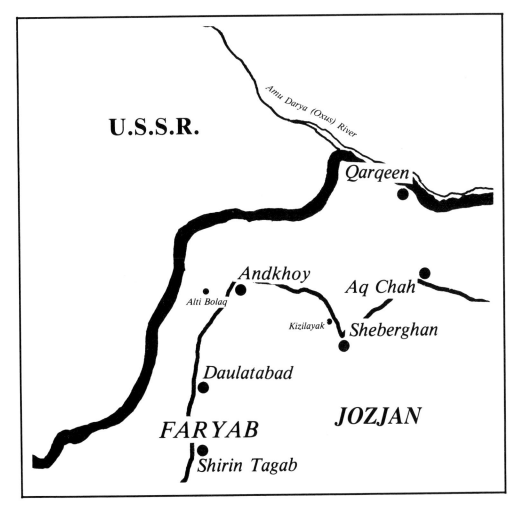

Andkhoy, in Faryab Province, lies seventy-five kilometres north of Sheberghan, and only some thirty kilometres from the Amu Darya (Oxus) River. Although the paved road ends here, the journey from Sheberghan is an easy one, taking a little over an hour by way of a newly constructed road, running almost parallel to the old track which winds around the patches of soft sand and dunes of this difficult terrain. In 1974, the dust-choked trip on this old road took a seemingly endless five hours. The scenery along the monotonous and fairly flat yet bumpy track is not exciting. The main vegetation is camel bush, that small round prickly shrub that is used for both winter fuel and fodder. Large tawny bustards perch on the rough wooden poles which

Camel bush on the old track from Sheberghan to Andkhoy

Colour Plate 76 *ALTI BOLAQ carpet in the Bokhara design. Note the rosettes in the main border guard, a typical feature of the classical Andkhoy production. (262 x 195cm).*

77

79

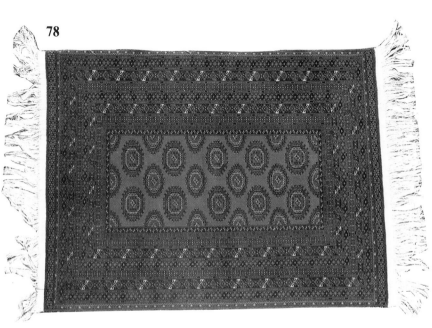

78

Colour Plate 77 An oldish ALTI BOLAQ carpet, the design of which is that of the Andkhoy Sulayman. It cannot be over-emphasised that the sole means of recognising and differentiating the Alti Bolaq production from much of the Andkhoy goods is 'in the back', i.e. in the weave. (295 x 219cm).

Courtesy Herr H. Engelhardt, Mannheim, West Germany

Colour Plate 78 A rug featuring the Andkhoy version of the Saruq design; in this piece natural dyestuffs have been used. (184 x 125cm).

Colour Plate 79 Part of a rug woven in Alti Bolaq which features the Baba Saqal design. (203 x 112cm).

poles which carry the single telephone wire to Andkhoy, or circle overhead in search of prey. Occasionally one sees a desert fox, or more likely a marmot, the small tailless rodent, darting across the track before disappearing into its burrow.

A few kilometres outside of Andkhoy is a small shrine, next to which live the keeper and his family. It is customary for travellers in either direction to give them a small coin in token of thanks for, or in the hope of, a safe journey. Turkomans from Andkhoy come out as far as this shrine to await an expected guest. After the traditional greetings and expressions of thanks to Allah for the safe arrival of their guest, they formally take over from the escort the responsibility for his safekeeping and lead the party into town. This touching custom is typical of Turkoman hospitality. On a journey in this part of the country, one is always accompanied by a Turkoman who hands you over to a known contact in the next town.

Andkhoy was one of the old Uzbek Khanates, dependent upon Bokhara and finally attached to Afghanistan by King Abdurahman in his attempt to unify the country in 1881.

Architecturally and scenically, it has little to recommend it. The town is frequently swept by blinding sand storms; water is brackish and the surrounding country is a barren and sandy waste. Yet Andkhoy has a marked atmosphere of its own and emanates that unrushed sense of purpose and dignified courtesy which is characteristic of its inhabitants.

Apart from carpet making, one of the major occupations is the Karaqul industry. These world-famous lambskins are sold at international auction in London and Leningrad every spring and autumn. Skins are graded by colour and quality, the black ones generally being the cheapest, and the golden the most expensive; quality within each colour is determined by the closeness and tightness of the curls and the size of the pelt. The most prized skins are those of unborn lambs, locally called *taqir,* and they are also marketed here. The buying of pelts, although demanding great skill, is often carried on as a sideline by the Andkhoy carpet dealers. In the spring, it is common to see a villager hawking his precious Karaqul pelts, tied up in an old kerchief. The purchaser salts the skins and then stacks them in the back of his shop, later to be resold to an exporter or to the government agency. Fortunes have been made and lost in this trade.

Sericulture is a secondary industry in Andkhoy, with the majority of the cocoons going to Japan. The premises of silkworm production in Andkhoy are reverently guarded, and many locals adhere to the ancient superstition which forbids strangers and women below a certain age from entering the lieu; however, today, it is only the non-Muslim whose baleful presence might prove harmful to the silkworms.

The principal inhabitants of Andkhoy are Uzbeks and Turkomans, with only a small proportion of the population comprising Pashtuns, Tajiks and Arabis. On bazaar days, Mondays and Thursdays, the local population is augmented by itinerant Pashtun traders, many of whom sell second-hand clothing or plastic sandals made in Kabul, and Arabi farmers from Daulatabad who have travelled all night across the dunes leading their camel caravans, the hindermost camel always supporting a bell and laden with melons or grapes. Carpet buyers and dealers from Kabul mingle with the throng in the Karim Baye Serai, where the carpet bazaar takes place, and elsewhere in town the various artisans, each in their own quarter, carry on a brisk business. There is a large section devoted to potters, whose wares include those huge earthenware jars, so important for the storage of water in these arid parts.

Turkoman settlements, as mentioned earlier, have existed in the north of Afghanistan for well over a century and a half, but it was not until the early 1920s, to escape the Bolshevik suppression of Turkestan, that a large number

of Ersari Turkomans crossed the Amu Darya River, only thirty-two kilometres distant from Andkhoy to seek refuge and a permanent home there.

Turkoman weavers in the Andkhoy region, all Ersaris from a variety of sub-clans, make several traditional designs. Uzbeks in this region, learning the craft of carpet making from these Turkomans, began making carpets in about 1960 and today contribute to a large extent to the Andkhoy production, the bulk of which comes from some twelve large villages around Andkhoy town. Another development and change from tradition is that, in the late 1960s, boys and youths — both Turkoman and Uzbek — started to weave. Today, many of the top quality pieces from Andkhoy are woven by men.

Of all the Turkomans settled in Afghan Turkestan, it is probably those of Andkhoy who are the quickest to set a trend or to adapt to change in the carpet market. It is almost paradoxical that, while being a proud and dignified people striving to maintain their own individuality, these Turkomans are also great copiers. They will copy the good as well as the bad. Probably the poverty and previous inaccessibility of the area have much to do with this. In terms of trade, this has its advantages, of course, as well as disadvantages. During the 1950s, the quality of the Andkhoy production was among the poorest in Afghanistan. Excluding the Tekke goods, the standing was Kunduz, Mazar, Aq Chah and lastly, Andkhoy and Qarqeen. Today, Andkhoy ranks with Kunduz in first place. Moreover, the top quality Andkhoy pieces, which today form about twenty per cent of the production, are still improving and can be compared with double-wefted Mauris from Herat.

One of the negative aspects is the fact that Andkhoy pieces, within each category, are now almost identical and it is virtually impossible to identify the clan origin of the weavers or to pinpoint with certitude the lieux of production — with the possible exception of the Alti Bolaq.

Turkoman village

Alti Bolaq

Two adjoining villages, upper and lower Alti Bolaq, form this important and well-known carpet-producing centre some ten kilometres south of Andkhoy. Alti Bolaq, mainly inhabited by Ersari Turkomans from the Qara clan, has given its name to both a design and to a superior quality of weave. Alas, today many rugs and carpets are fraudulently sold under this name. The traditional Alti Bolaq design is known as the Bokhara design, or *kar-i-sefide*. Both the primary and secondary *guls* are very similar to the Tekke *gul* but unlike the Tekke design, the primary *guls* are not joined by a grid line. The borders nearly always feature the large rosette motif associated with Andkhoy goods. (See Colour Plate 76).

The *fil-pai* motif, not uncommon in the Alti Bolaq production, is often a smaller octagon than the traditional Afghan elephant foot and is identical to the new Sulayman *gul*.

The *Sygyrnme* design so often seen in the ends of carpets featuring the Bokhara design does not always appear in the traditional Alti Bolaq. (See Colour Plates 77, 78, and 79).

Alti Bolaq Characteristics:

General: Firm and supple handle. Clean back, clearly ridged; very regular tight knotting. Double wefted. Mainly synthetic dyestuffs.

Designs: Mostly Bokhara but *fil-pai* not uncommon; though quite frequently have a smaller version of the *fil-pai* (elephant's

78a

Colour Plate 78a A classical SARUQ rug made in Marchark. The field is of a deep aubergine colour. Note the irregularities in the secondary guls. (193 x 143cm).

Shir Khosrow Paiwand

79a

79b

Colour Plates 79a, 79b A section of an old TAGHAN carpet made in Labijar, which displays a marked Saltuq influence. Note the typical Labijar kilim, measuring 13cm, also the incidence of light indigo, which gives a duck-egg blue effect, and the wide goat hair selvedge. (272 x 231cm).

Courtesy Shir Khosrow Paiwand

80a

80b

Colour Plate 80a *Old SULAYMAN. (See insert on page 93). Both the narrow and repetitive border as well as the kilim suggest that this piece was made in the Sheberghan district. (188 x 107cm).*

Courtesy Shir Khosrow Paiwand

Colour Plate 80b. *Old SULAYMAN. A rich brown field obtained from madder mixed with walnut, and having no secondary guls. A band containing green runs across the second gul from the bottom., The incompleted* fil-pai *gul at the top is an example of the weaver using her dyed yarn to maximum capacity! (196 x 102cm)*

Courtesy Shir Khosrow Paiwand

foot) design. Karaqul wool; increasing use of imported mill-spun yarn dyed red for the field; and undyed for white motifs. Plain white *kilims*.

Colours: Red, indigo, white, also orange and sometimes green.

Warps: 2-ply undyed grey Karaqul wool, increasing tendency to use imported blended machine-spun white yarn.

Wefts: Usually one cotton and one 2-ply wool weft dyed red.

Selvedges: Red, indigo; blanket stitch.

Knots: Asymmetric.

Sizes: Rugs of 2 and 2.5m², also 9m² and 12m² (200 x 100, 200 x 125cm, also 350 x 250 and 400 x 300cm).

The Sulaymans

The Sulaymans are a large Ersari sub-clan found throughout Afghan Turkestan and especially in the Andkhoy region, although they produce carpets in three other areas, namely, Mazar, Kunduz and Aq Chah.

The Andkhoy Sulayman *gul,* as well as its secondary motif, is easily recognisable in current production (see Colour Plate 82). The border often displays the large rosette motif. As in all Andkhoy goods, a bright red, tending to an orange tone, is favoured, and white Kandahari wool dyed red is increasingly being used for the field. The Andkhoy Sulayman *gul* is now widely copied by other groups, as, indeed, the Sulayaman himself copies the Bokhara *gul.*

The Sulayman *gul* from Aq Chah is similar to that of Andkhoy, though more crowded and less distinct, but the secondary motif is the same. The main difference lies in their borders (see Colour Plate 81). The Aq Chah Sulayman is also more red in overall tone.

The Sulayman production from the Mazar and Kunduz areas is quite different from that of either Andkhoy or Aq Chah. The *gul* from the former always contains the 'Christmas tree' motif common to the Dalis and old Qarqeens. This motif is described by some Turkomans as the 'spine and rib' motif (when the design is seen from above, this in fact, becomes apparent). Sometimes, especially in the older goods, the *fil-pai* motif is encased in a panel. The numerous border guards, the deeper red tones and the undyed wefts make the Sulayman carpets from Mazar and Kunduz quite distinct.

The fact that carpets woven in the above four areas by the same sub-clan of Sulayman Turkomans are of such diversity of design is another interesting example of how the creative impulse has adapted itself to various local and neighbouring influences, as well as, perhaps, the effects of commercialisation. (See Colour Plates 80 and 82).

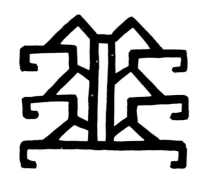

Sulayman gul, *variously called 'inverted ribcage', 'spine and rib', 'pine tree' or 'Christmas tree' motif.*

Kizilayak (Andkhoy)

The Kizilayaks of Andkhoy, like other Turkomans here, tend to weave the design currently in fashion. However, when making carpets which feature the elephant foot, they use the Sulayman version of this motif. Kizilayak pieces can easily be identified by the classic Kizilayak motif (see detail page 99) which appears in either one or two of the border guards. The Andkhoy Kizilayaks, unlike the Sheberghan Kizilayaks, often produce large and oversize pieces.

Ghaba Saqal (sometimes Baba Saqal). Both mean 'old man's beard'.

The Ghaba Saqals, another widely scattered Ersari sub-clan, also contribute to the Andkhoy production. The striking Ghaba Saqal *gul* is now only woven in Andkhoy and Aq Chah. The Andkhoy Ghaba Saqal design is the more elaborate and multicoloured, with red, orange, gold, cream, royal blue, indigo and sometimes green. (See Colour Plate 83).

The Aq Chah Ghaba Saqal rug is less vivid; the main colours being red, indigo and white, with sometimes the *gul* of undyed natural grey Karaqul wool.

Charchangi

The Charchangi is another Ersari sub-clan producing carpets and rugs in the Andkhoy region.

The bold Charchangi design, so full of character, is rarer today than it was even in the mid-1970s. The same design is woven in the Soviet Turkestan factories where its interpretation is very monotonous, and is exported to the West under the name of Kizilayak. However, every Charchangi I have questioned has vehemently claimed this pattern as his own, and by the same token, no Kizilayak known to me in Afghanistan has ever laid claim to it.

Like the dispersed and varied products of the Sulaymans, the Charchangi of Aq Chah weave a totally different design from the Andkhoy Charchangi (see Colour Plate 84).

Typical roadside shrine

Chaker

Another typical clan design which has become rare in the Andkhoy market is the *kheshti (*or brick) *gul* of the Chakers, another Ersari sub-clan. This simple and unmistakable square *gul* is almost never seen in today's production, having gone out of fashion in the early 1970s. The Chakers presently weave either the Bokhara design or the elephant foot Sulayman *gul*.

Other Designs in the Andkhoy Production

As seen above, the principal designs in the Andkhoy production, with its vast interrelated community of different tribes, clans and sub-clans, are the elephant foot and the Bokhara *gul,* or *kar-i-sefide*. There are a number of other designs (see page 118), however, which appear significantly in the Andkhoy production. Except for the Saruq, these miscellaneous motifs bear the name of the design itself and *not* a clan name.

The Saruq design appears in the Andkhoy production, but it is a copy of the traditional Saruq from the area of Maruchark (see page 29). The coarser weave, the hairier back and the thicker and less supple handle of an Andkhoy Saruq could never be mistaken for the genuine product. Moreover, in the Andkhoy Saruqs, the blue is quite often lighter than the traditional dark indigo seen in the authentic pieces from Maruchark.

The *alma gul* (apple blossom) is a popular design in the Andkhoy production and is made by all and sundry, though traditionally this design (often called Beshiri) is made by the Hassan Mangali sub-clan who are more numerous in both Kunduz and Mazar than in Andkhoy. Generally speaking,

81a

81b

81c

Colour Plate 81a Old SULAYMAN from Andkhoy. This piece is noteworthy for a variety of now-unusual attributes. The field is of madder mixed with walnut, resulting in a warm pale tobacco-brown, and no secondary guls. The centre of the primary guls is of kermes *(cochineal). Both skirts are decorated with a simple four-diamond motif unusual in Sulaymans. The incidence of undyed brown wool contrasting with the indigo makes for an uncommon yet harmonious colour combination. (240 x 130cm).*

Shir Khosrow Paiwand

Colour Plates 81b, 81c A section of classical old SULAYMAN carpet, dating from circa 1930, from Kunduz Province. (284 x 201cm).

Shir Khosrow Paiwand

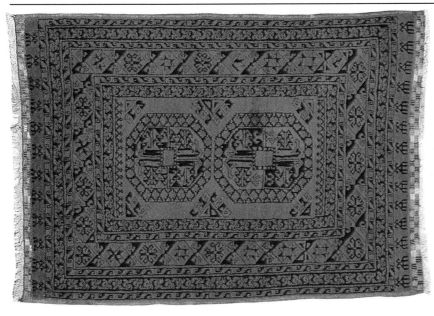

Colour Plate 80 *Oldish SULAYMAN rug from Kunduz. The 'inverted ribcage' or 'pine tree' motif appears in the quadrants of the primary gul (see page 114). This motif does not appear in either the Andkhoy or Aq Chah Sulayman production. Apart from the deep red associated with rugs from the Kunduz area, it is not uncommon for the primary gul to be enclosed in a panel, thus obviating the need for a secondary gul.*

Colour Plate 81 *SULAYMAN rug from Aq Chah. The primary gul, whilst similar to that of the Andkhoy Sulayman, is usually more crowded and less clear. Note the border, which is so typically Aq Chah. (199 x 155cm).*

Colour Plate 82 *Typical ANDKHOY SULAYMAN rug. The design is typical but not the contrast. (198 x 128cm).*

Courtesy Herr H. Engelhardt, Mannheim, West Germany

81 / 82

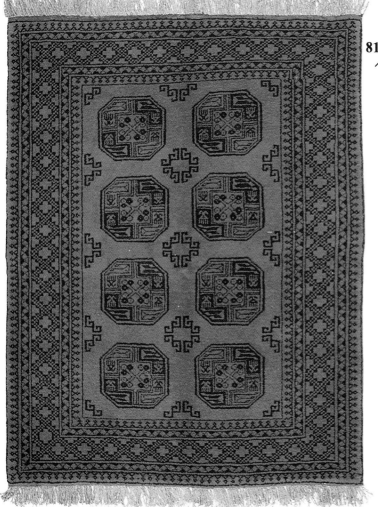

Andkhoy carpets bearing the *alma gul* design are rather bright in colouring. The reds are orange in tone and orange, gold, cream, royal blue, indigo and green are commonly used.

The *waziri* design, described on page 102, is also found in the Andkhoy production, where it has now become a classic. The best executed and the most elaborate form of this design comes from here today and is made by all and sundry.

The *narche gashtai,* literally the 'wandering design', is the name given locally to all those non-traditional designs which appear in the Andkhoy production. As with the increased use of non-traditional colours, these designs came into existence for several reasons, the main one being propaganda put out by the Carpet Exporters' Guild.

This Guild was set up by the Afghan Ministry of Commerce in the mid-1960s with the aim of improving quality and increasing carpet exports. Instead of keeping to the excellent old traditional designs and colours, and concentrating on improving quality, mistaken enthusiasm led the Guild to urge weavers to use non-traditional colours and to execute 'new' designs. This resulted in a travesty of Turkoman professional dignity, together with an output of cheap-looking goods whose popularity was generally of short duration. One such example was the *narche kafqazi*, or Caucasian design, introduced into local Turkoman production in the late 1960s. During 1970-75 it was very popular in some Western markets (where anything goes for a time) but by the end of the decade it had virtually disappeared from the current Andkhoy production.

In about 1973, one began to see in the Andkhoy market a small number of carpets and rugs made entirely from natural undyed wool. These pieces generally have the Bokhara design in the field, though often the borders are untypical. This pallid, insipid carpet is usually bought by those whose taste and appreciation of Afghan carpets is still in the embryonic stage and who are looking merely for a floor covering which will blend with the existing furnishings. A few of these pieces are now also being made in Aq Chah by various weavers.

Another interesting feature of the Andkhoy production is a growing tendency, which began in about 1974, to resuscitate old Turkoman designs which they used to weave decades ago in what was then an area under the control of the Emir of Bokhara. These are not by any means restricted only to Ersari designs. For instance, both the *kepsi gul* (see Colour Plate 85) and the overall repetitive *gul donneh* (see drawing) of the Yamouds is appearing with increasing frequency, as is the Beshiri *boteh* design, seen in some of the older carpets and rugs from the Kunduz area. This production, as yet small, for it barely exceeds 400m² per month, is of fine quality and natural dyestuffs are extensively used.

A major change which took place about 1970 in the Andkhoy production, and which caught on rapidly, was the introduction of the cotton weft. Today, about ninety per cent of the Andkhoy production is blighted by this departure from tradition which has so altered the texture of Afghan Turkoman goods. Albeit, the general quality of Andkhoy goods has increased substantially over the years and the indications are that this happy trend will continue.

The following table shows the major change that has taken place in the overall Andkhoy production regarding designs:

	1968	1978
Elephant foot	65%	25%
Bokhara or *kar-i-sefide*	25%	70%
Others: Andkhoy Saruq, *waziri, narche gashtai,* Caucasian, Beshiri *alma gul,* Beshiri *boteh,* etc.	10%	5%

gul donneh

Andkhoy Characteristics:

It will be appreciated that in such a large and varied production as that of Andkhoy, it is impossible to give more than a broad cursory list of characteristics.

General: Firm handle, somewhat harder than the traditional Afghan Turkoman rug because of cotton wefts in the majority of pieces. Generally clean back and tight knotting; less so in cheaper qualities. Double wefted, synthetic dyestuffs: a small but growing tendency to revert to natural dyestuffs in best goods only.

Designs: Bokhara *gul, fil-pai,* large rosette in border.

Colours: Orange, red, indigo, white, green.

Warps: 2-ply undyed Karaqul wool, though a growing tendency to use white imported machine-spun blended yarn.

Wefts: Usually one cotton and one 2-ply wollen weft dyed red.

Selvedges: Red, indigo or royal blue; blanket stitch.

Knots: Asymmetric.

Sizes: Carpet sizes mostly 6m² (300cm x 200cm) though all carpet sizes are made. 4m² (240cm x 170cm) rare. Rug sizes: 2m² or 2.5m² (200cm x 100cm or 200cm x 125cm). Runners also made.

83

Colour Plate 83 A GHABA SAQAL rug. *The colouring used in this piece is far from being traditional. (199 x 102cm).*

Colour Plate 84 An Andkhoy CHARCHANGI carpet. *(288 x 211cm).*

Colour Plate 85 YAMOUD rug with kepsi gul. *Indigo and other natural dyestuffs have been used in the making of this piece which was woven in Andkhoy by an Ersari Oumar weaver. (Approx. 200 x 50cm).*

84

85

83a

84a

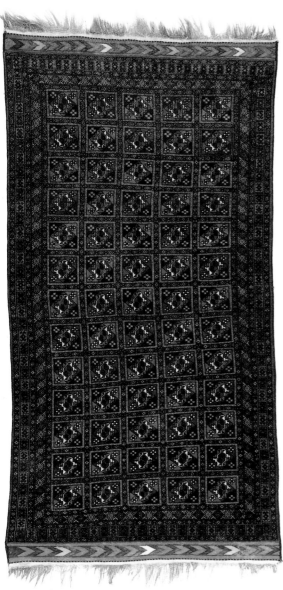

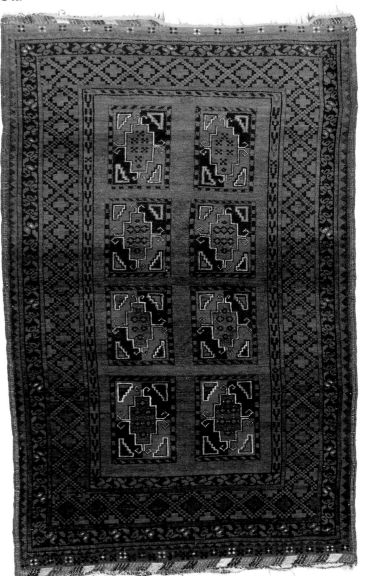

Colour Plate 83a *An ALTI BOLAQ carpet with an extraordinary detailed* aina gul *(literally, mirror). This motif is popular among the Yamoud Turkomans of northeast Iran and is also found in some Jamshidi and other Beluch-type productions, both in rugs and khourgines. Nowadays this design is rarely seen in Turkoman production, although it is being resuscitated in refugee camps. In the above carpet, hand-spun yarn, some undyed, some dyed with natural dyestuffs and some with synthetic, e.g. the gold. (212 x 118cm).*

Shir Khosrow Paiwand

Colour Plate 84a *A typical CHAKER rug (see page 104). This piece is from the Aq Chah region and dates from circa 1945. (180 x 116cm).*

Shir Khosrow Paiwand

Chapter 10
Daulatabad (Faryab), Maimana, Qaisar, and Sharkh (Tekke) Production

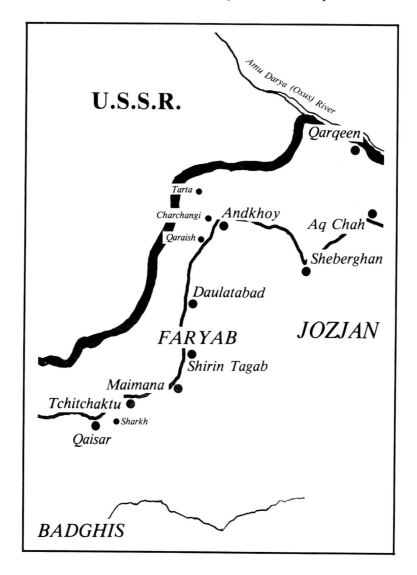

The Daulatabad (Faryab) Production

Daulatabad, approximately half-way between Andkhoy and Maimana, has given its name to one of the better known qualities of Afghan Turkoman carpets.

The town itself is small. Not more than about forty shops line its newly reconstructed main street, and most of these are open only on Sundays and

Wednesdays when the bi-weekly bazaar is held. On these two days, the main street is thronged with people from the surrounding villages which make up this administrative district.

There are twenty-one villages in the area, of which only three are Turkoman: Qaraish, Charchangi and Tarta. The inhabitants of these three villages number between five and six thousand souls, and of these, less than half actually weave, and even then not always full time. Thus, it is obvious that Turkoman production from this area is only a fraction of that sold under the name of Daulatabad; another fraction is made by the Uzbeks of this area. The remaining production comes from elsewhere and is misrepresented as that of Daulatabad.

The early Turkoman inhabitants are thought to have come from the USSR some seventy years ago, with more recent immigration in the early 1920s and since. It is these Turkomans who produced the well-known Daulatabad quality carpet with the traditional *fil-pai* design. Today, this design is associated with the new Sulayman proudction (see Colour Plate 82). This is what may have given rise to the frequent — but quite erroneous — use of the term 'Daulatabad' for all carpets with the elephant foot design. Another typical characteristic of the old Daulatabad was the absence of a secondary *gul*.

Apart from the firm, yet supple texture, and the clean, ridged back, another distinguishing feature of this carpet was its lovely browny-salmon colour, acquired after a relatively short time, and which one associates with some of the older Tekke pieces from Barmazid and Sharkh (see Colour Plates 46 and 47). This colour was probably obtained by mixing natural dyestuffs, such as madder or pomegranate peel with chlorozol dyestuffs, no longer manufactured.

Alas, these old Daulatabads are no longer offered for sale in the local bazaar; neither are the mats with the Bokhara design, which until eighteen years ago were an appreciable part of the production of this area. These goods are no longer being made.

The vast majority of modern Daulatabads consists of carpets ranging from 6m^2 to 12m^2 (300cm x 200cm to 400cm x 300cm), with the *fil-pai* motif or the Bokhara *gul*, in approximately equal proportions.

Rugs in sizes of 2m^2 to 3m^2 (200cm x 100cm to 200cm x 150cm) and runners are also woven. Frequently the designs, on either a red or a blue ground, contain a *gul* reminiscent of a small Saruq *gul*. Camel hair is sometimes used.

The current carpet scene is a fast-changing one, and there is no doubt that the importance and role of the bazaar in Daulatabad have greatly diminished. The vast majority of today's carpets and runners made here are spoken for while still on the loom, and no sooner are they finished than they find their way to the warehouses of those few exporters in Kabul who specialise in this production. However, the odd pieces may still be found in Andkhoy on market day, probably because of a broken agreement between weaver and dealer.

Another example of change is that the use of madder is being reintroduced, though only a small proportion of pieces. Again, the preponderance of the Bokhara design in modern Daulatabads is probably only a reflection of current fashion, a trend which could and would be reversed if fashion changes.

Today, an important part of the production of this area is the Daulatabad prayer rug (see Colour Plate 86). This is a recent development, dating from about 1963. The origin of this comparatively new production is interesting, as it is another instance of the change taking place in the carpet industry of Afghanistan. Several *mullahs* (religious leaders) brought back from their pilgrimage to Mecca some cheap machine-made cotton prayer rugs, produced by the hundreds of thousands, depicting the sacred shrine in gaudy

86

87

Colour Plate 86 DAULATABAD *prayer rug with camel hair. This piece is very typical of this production. (130 x 78cm).*

Author's collection

Colour Plate 87 Stylised PURDAH from QAISAR. These do not pass through the Maimana bazaar commercially, but are mainly marketed in Kabul. (205 x 149cm).

representation. One of the *mullahs* copied the design in *namads* (felt rugs), which he sold easily, and he persuaded his wife and members of his family to start weaving a prayer rug of that design. The idea caught on and by 1972, the production, although considerable, could barely meet the foreign demand.

This prayer rug became popular in European markets probably because of its newness. However, the demand is now lessening, undoubtedly due to the lowering of general quality. In addition, the tendency to use cheap blue dyes instead of the traditional indigo, which often results in a royal blue changing into a muddy grey after a short period of oxidation, and the recent unfortunate introduction of Pakistani machine-spun yarn containing man-made fibres, have resulted in a loss of confidence in these goods.

Of the other eighteen villages in the Daulatabad district mentioned earlier, twelve are inhabited by Pashtuns and Arabis, a tribe of Arab stock who virtually do no weaving, and the remaining six villages by Uzbeks who started weaving on a very small scale some fifteen years ago.

There is no doubt that the lowering of the standards of Daulatabad goods is due to the emergence of the Uzbek weaver. Encouraged by indiscriminating foreign buyers for whom price is paramount for their aggressive marketing policies with double pricing and phoney discounts, the Uzbek weaver, to a large extent, is responsible for besmirching an honourable reputation. On the other hand, one can hope that he will improve, as he has in other places, notably in Andkhoy.

The Daulatabad Uzbek weave is, in the main, much coarser and less regular than that of the Turkoman, and often suffers from such a poorly spun weft so tightly beaten down that the back is as hard as plywood, and often the pile is woefully short of wool — if wool it is! In addition, the too-tightly packed back makes for a tendency to crookedness.

Daulatabad Characteristics:

General: Firm and supple handle. Clean ridged back; tight knotting, double wefted, all Karaqul wool, synthetic dyestuffs. Plain white *kilim*.
Designs: Bokhara, *fil-pai* and Daulatabad *gul*.
Colours: Red, indigo, royal blue, white; camel hair.
Warps: 2-ply Karaqul wool, increasing use of imported machine spun yarn.
Wefts: One cotton, one wool, both dyed red.
Selvedges: Red/indigo; blanket stitch.
Knots: Asymmetric
Sizes: Prayer rugs, 2m x 1m, 6m² and 12m² (300 cm x 200cm and 400cm x 300cm).

The Maimana Production

In and around Maimana, the capital of Faryab, the westernmost province of Afghan Turkestan and a former Uzbek Khanate of some importance, there are relatively few Turkomans and as a carpet centre, it is of no relevance. One hears the expression 'Maimana goods', but this refers to carpets from other small centres of the west of this capital. In Maimana itself, there are a half dozen or more dealers who have shops, but with a limited stock of carpets and rugs. Occasionally, one finds a few so-called 'Daulatabad' prayer rugs from Shirin Tagab or some coarse and cheap rugs made in the picturesque regions around Shirak, Darzab and Bel Cherag, but production from these districts is

Maimana — a feast laid ready for Jeshun (King's birthday) a national holiday

Maimana

Turkomans crossing river at Maimana

extremely limited and the majority of pieces, in any case, are made for the commercial market and are sent directly to Andkhoy or to Kabul. One may perhaps also find in the Maimana bazaar an old Tekke piece from Sharkh, which production is described in this chapter, or a Tchitchaktu.

The main goods offered for sale are the flat-woven *khourjeens* and *kilims*, which feature so strongly in everyday Afghan life, and are made by all tribes throughout the area. The Maimana *kilim*, traditionally woven by Uzbeks, is still being made today by these same people and also being copied by Aimaqs. These *kilims,* which contain a good amount of gold or yellow, are generally woven in sizes of 8m², or more, which is larger than most *kilims* woven in Afghanistan.

Bazaar days in Maimana are Mondays and Thursdays, but little business concerning carpets or woven goods takes place. *Kilims,* of course, are the principal items offered, with an increasing number of Hazaragi *kilims* from Sari-Pul and locally made *khourjeens* and *namads*.

A rather interesting product from Maimana is the *sadranji*. This is a flat-woven fabric made entirely from cotton by the inmates of the Maimana prison. These same pieces are also made by prisoners in Kabul and other major provincial capitals. The *sadranjis* range in size from 6m² to 12m², or larger. Colours are usually pastel shades of green, blue, pink and red, and the designs are simple and geometric. Cotton *sadranji* prayer mats are also made in the Maimana prison.

Some thirty kilometres west of Maimana in an arid, flat plain lies the *woleswali* of Almar. The population here is mainly Uzbek, with a few Tajik and Pashtun villages, and one small village of some twenty Ersari Turkoman families. Production from the Almar district is insignificant, consisting mostly of rugs, *kilims* and *khourjeens,* which are marketed in Andkhoy or directly in Kabul. Very few pieces from here are sold in the Maimana bazaar.

Shirin Tagab

The small town of Shirin Tagab, forty kilometres north of Maimana is inhabited largely by Uzbeks. While rugs are being made here in increasing numbers, Shirin Tagab cannot yet be reckoned as an important carpet-producing centre. Most of the goods made here are rather coarse and mainly in rug sizes, with whatever design happens to be currently in fashion. Thus, at the height of the popularity of the Daulatabad prayer rug, this design was predominant, giving way in the late 1970s to *kar-i-sefide*. Weaving in Shirin Tagab is a comparatively new development, dating back only to the early 1970s, so there is reason to hope that the standard will improve.

Bazaar days are Mondays and Thursdays, but the carpet section is insignificant.

Qaisar

Typical valley cultivation in an arid country

Travelling westward and crossing three wide, shallow river beds which are dry for most of the year, one reaches Qaisar. Predominantly an Uzbek town, Qaisar is of growing importance as a minor carpet-producing centre. A small number of carpets and rugs had been produced here for some time, but it was only in the 1970s that the industry increased markedly, when a number of the local population took to weaving as a result of the disastrous drought of 1970-71. By 1978, the Qaisar production had come into its own, and presently the goods from here are easily recognisable by both their irregular weave and their designs.

Designs are generally a non-traditional, bastardised form of the classical *purdah,* in soft colours with old gold and browny-pink predominant. (See Colour Plate 87).

These *purdahs* do not pass through the Maimana bazaar commercially, but are mainly marketed in Kabul. Bazaar days are Mondays and Thursdays, with an expanding carpet section.

Qaisar Characteristics:

General:	Fairly firm handle. Variable back, generally untidy and hairy; knotting tending to be loose. Double wefted, synthetic dyestuffs except for occasional madders.
Designs:	Bastardised *purdah,* and Caucasian designs; also, new and non-traditional designs; usually plain white *kilim.*
Colours:	Indigo, old gold, browny-pink, muddy green, fawn, brown.
Warps:	Increasing use of 2-ply white imported machine-spun blended wool. Also off-white Hazaragi and Ghilzai wool; sometimes silk.
Wefts:	2-ply undyed Karaqul wool; frequently one cotton undyed or brown weft.
Selvedges:	Indigo, brown; blanket stitch.
Knots:	Asymmetric.
Sizes:	Variable, most rug sizes.

The Tekke Turkoman Production from Sharkh

Sharkh is a small town several kilometres south of the northern Circular Route, between Qaisar and Tchitchaktu, and accessible by a rough and sandy track winding through scattered villages and grazing grounds. Bazaar days are Fridays and Tuesdays, but no carpet bazaar is held in Sharkh; periodically, all the production is sent directly to one single dealer in Kabul, who is a Tekke himself.

The Tekkes of Sharkh live in about one hundred houses grouped together in one section of the town. They are a close-knit society whose main form of livelihood is farming.

The Tekkes here weave carpets of various size with all hand-spun wool, though there is a recent tendency to use blended machine-spun yarn for the warps. They use both synthetic and natural dyestuffs. A considerable proportion of the Sharkh carpets displays the small Tekke *gul* or the larger *akhel gul;* the Saruq design is also woven, and recently a few *purdahs* have appeared. The Sharkh goods are always double wefted. The overall classical designs are similar to those of the Barmazids, though with variations in the details of the intricate border guards. This similarity holds true for weaving techniques, and the general appearances of front and back, as well as the handle. (See Colour Plates 46 and 47).

The majority of the inhabitants of Sharkh and the nearby villages are Pashtuns, Uzbeks, Aimaqs and Tajiks, and almost all of these people have become weavers over the last few years. They learned this craft from the Tekkes, and a few of them have now reached such a high standard that their work is indistinguishable from that of the Tekkes, an illustration of how tribes with no weaving tradition can, by close association and under Turkoman tutelage and influence, develop high degrees of skill in this art.

Many carpets and rugs that are sold in western markets under the name of Sharkh do not actually come from here, and of those that do, a majority are

not even Tekke weaves. These pseudo-Tekke Sharkhs are often recognisable by the fact that the upper weft is cotton. Real Tekke production from Sharkh cannot possibly exceed two hundred to three hundred pieces a year.

Tekke Turkoman Characteristics:

General: Firm supple handle, clean ridged back of regular weave; tight knotting. Double wefted, synthetic and natural dyes.

Designs: Small octagonal Tekke *gul, akhel gul,* recently the *purdah;* some Saruq *guls.* All Karaqul wool, white motifs of Kandahari wool. Plain white *kilim.*

Colour: Red, indigo and white.

Warps: 2-ply Karaqul wool, undyed; recent introduction of imported 3-ply machine-spun yarn.

Wefts: 1-ply Karaqul wool, dyed red.

Selvedges: Mostly red, some indigo; blanket stitch.

Knots: Asymmetric.

Sizes: Mainly carpets of 6m² to 12m², a few of 4m² and rug sizes; no prayer rugs.

CHAPTER 11
Beluch and Beluch-type Production

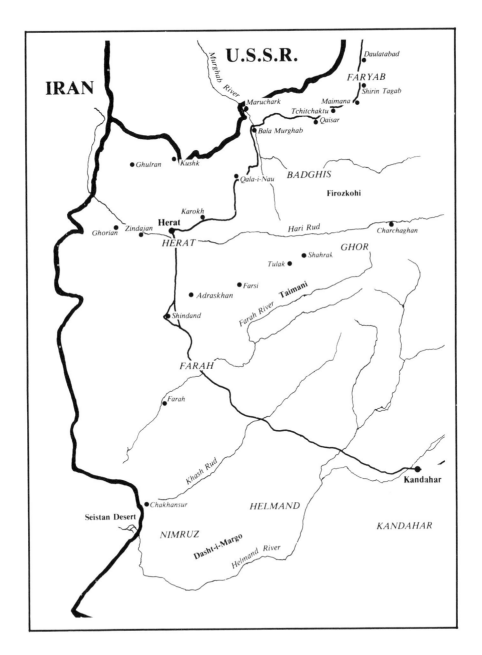

The name Beluch, strictly speaking, does not refer to a single ethnic group, but to all those semi-sedentary and sedentary peoples living in Beluchistan, a large

Nomadic tents

A nomadic group in the foothills of the rolling steppes

area of western Afghanistan which also extends into southern Pakistan and Iran.

The Beluchs can be divided into two main ethnic groups; the Rukhshanis and the Brahuis, numbering some three hundred thousand people with well over one hundred clans and sub-clans. The Rukhshanis traditionally originated from an area south of the Caspian Sea and speak a language similar to that of western Iran, while the Brahuis are said to have migrated to the western deserts of Afghanistan from northern India after the Aryan invasion some five thousand years ago. Their language is quite different from any other Beluch group.

Throughout western Afghanistan, there are nomadic, sedentary and semi-sedentary Beluch tribes and sub-clans who make carpets and rugs commercially. In addition, there is a widespread non-Beluch population, also sedentary or nomadic, whose large and varied production of rugs and carpets resembles in one or more ways the goods produced by the actual Beluchs. It is this production by the non-Beluch weavers that is here called the Beluch-type. In the trade, however, no distinction is made between these two productions, both types being called 'Herat Beluch'.

Two general characteristics of the Beluch and Beluch-type goods are that they are made entirely of wool (the Beluch production in Iran as a rule has cotton warps and wefts), and many pieces contain the weaver's hallmark. This unique feature is usually a large dot of a very bright colour extraneous to the overall design placed either in the border or the field. As with the Turkoman production, all weaving is done on horizontal looms and the asymmetric knot is used throughout; unlike the Turkomans, only women do the weaving. A common feature of both the Beluch and the Beluch-type carpet is that it tends to be very dark, long and narrow. Wool for both productions comes principally from the Beluchi and Ghilzai breeds of sheep in the south, and the Karaqul in the north of Herat. Bi-annual shearing, carding, spinning and dyeing techniques are similar to those used by the Turkomans. The dyes are principally synthetic though with some exceptions.

The geographic region, wherein lie the centres of production of the Beluch and Beluch-type goods, covers approximately the western third of Afghanistan, that is, the area west of a line drawn from Tchitchaktu in the north down to the Pakistan border. This extensive region contains the picturesque and remote mountains of Ghor Province, the rolling plains of Badghis and Herat Provinces, as well as the arid deserts of the Seistan. These areas are sparsely populated, though large flocks of sheep move slowly across the unfolding hills to fresh pasturage. The large flocks usually belong to a wealthy Pashtun *maldar* or flockmaster, or a Beluch Khan, who employ either a very young or a very old shepherd to supervise their 'wealth on the hoof'. A shepherd tending a flock of four hundred sheep is paid a monthly salary of the equivalent of £12.50 (at the time of writing). He is constantly on the move, adapting himself to the extremes of temperatures and systematically guiding his flock to known watering places and on to newer grazing. Buried in his tattered clothing he carries the hard, sun-dried lumps of soured milk, called *grut,* which is his main food.

He and his animals are guarded by the ubiquitous and popularly called *kuchi* dog (*sag-i-ramah*) those large fierce mastiffs whose broad chest and fleetness of foot are more than a match for wolves and other predators.

From late summer to early winter, the odd ram or ewe is partially painted with bright colours, usually blue, magenta, henna or green. This is done to animals in the peak of condition, to ward off the Evil Eye, other disease, or a would-be thief. The theory behind this widespread custom is that the Evil Eye is deflected by the gaudy colours, and so will not alight on the prized animals.

Sag-i-ramah dog herding sheep

Much of the south-western region of Afghanistan is chronically arid. Wells of often brackish water are scattered here and there to be used when the water courses dry up in the blistering heat of summer and autumn. Water is raised in big leather buckets, or, a recent innovation, buckets made from old rubber lorry tyres.

From July through September the 'Wind of 120 Days' blasts down the broad corridor along the Iran-Afghanistan border from Herat to the Seistan, bringing with it vicious dust storms and temperatures that have been recorded as high as 48⁰C at midnight. The southernmost region of this area borders on the *Dasht-i-Margo,* the Desert of Death, which forms part of the great world deserts sweeping from central India to Morocco.

It will be appreciated that in such an extensive geographic area as this, with extremes not only in altitude, physical features and climate, but also in the complexity of different ethnic groups and tribes with no uniform culture, it is impossible to give a precise description of the carpet production from this region. This is further complicated by the fact that there are duplications of totally unrelated tribal and place names; many of these people are on the move, especially from February to November, and are seldom in the same place for two consecutive months, and that various tribes found west of the Tchitchaktu line are also found in the eastern region of Afghanistan, where they do not weave commercially.

Furthermore, designs typical of a particular area are now being copied elsewhere, and new designs or modifications are constantly being introduced. These trends are increasing as roads are opened and travel to remote places becomes easier for both itinerant traders and village populations. Moreover, market forces and the ever-changing local economic climate influence the size and quality of production. Thus, we will see yet further gradual changes taking place in the Afghan carpet industry. The marketing centre for goods made in this vast area of western Afghanistan is Herat.

Drawing water from a deep well

Herat, a Marketing Centre

The great oasis of the city of Herat lies in one of the richest and most fertile provinces of Afghanistan. With a history going back over two thousand five hundred years, this ancient city was one of the sites chosen by Alexander the Great for his first Alexandria in Afghanistan. Occupied by successive waves of conquering armies from Iran and central Asia, it finally ceded to Arab invaders, who were swept into Afghanistan on the engulfing tide of Islam. Herat, even in the tenth century drew philosophers and scholars from all over the Islamic world, to argue theosophy with the great Sufi mystic Abdullah Ansari, among others, in the shadow of the venerable Friday Mosque, still one of the most beautiful buildings of Afghanistan.

Herat did not escape the Mongol invasions of Genghis Khan nor the decimating armies of Tamerlane, who razed the city to the ground in 1381. On the ruins of Herat one of Tamerlane's sons rebuilt a city equal in splendour to his father's capital in Samarkand. The fifteenth century in Herat produced monuments of architectural, artistic and intellectual grandeur that made it a vigorous centre of learning and among the most resplendent capitals of the Islamic world. During this Golden Age the Persian poet Jami and the miniaturist Behzad were among the two hundred or more artists, musicians and men of learning gathered at the Royal Court.

The traditional artistic skills of Herati craftsmen are still evident today in the ateliers of the tile makers, the gold and silversmiths, the silk weavers, and the glass blowers who make the famous delicate blue glass vases, goblets, beads and other ornaments.

Herat mosque

Four of the original nine minarets which are part of the Musalla complex designed and built by Queen Gawhar Shah (daughter-in-law of Tamerlane) in 1417

Herat is now a teeming city, with men from all tribes of Afghanistan mingling in the streets. However, the distinct accent of the true Herati, as well as his charm, cunning and business acumen, is unmistakable. And nowhere does he appear more at home than in the Herat carpet bazaar, for although it is small it is highly significant as it is the main marketing centre for all the Beluch and Beluch-type goods that are brought to it from the southernmost desert of Afghanistan as well as from the mountainous region of Ghor and the fertile plans of Ghulran in the north-west of the country. It has been the practice for some years to teach long-term convicts in the larger provincial prisons the craft of carpet making. Herat is no exception, and up to the early 1970s the prisoners of Herat gaol made carpets similar in both design and colouring to a type of Iranian carpet from Meshed across the border. These pieces were coarse and were sold to the public or to dealers through the prison shop. Today in Herat long-term prisoners make a rather coarse double-wefted carpet having the Tekke *gul,* which in design only resembles the Mauri of Herat.

The Turkoman Carpets of Herat

The Mauri Carpet from Herat and Ghorian

The Tekkes who settled in Herat have continued their tradition of weaving carpets and rugs of great fineness. They have given their stamp to the Herat Turkoman production which is called the Mauri. The word 'Mauri' means 'of, or from Merv', the city in Soviet Turkestan whence these weavers came, and although primarily Tekke, also included members of the Yamoud and Saruq tribes.

Thus, the term Mauri refers both to the design, the small classical octagonal Tekke *gul,* and also to the weave of these carpets, which is very fine, often with well over five hundred knots per linear metre of warp, and usually single wefted. Unfortunately, other pieces, also often single wefted and with the same *gul,* notably the Jamshidi rug, are produced in this area and sold under the name of Mauri.

Over the last few years, the range of Mauri designs has expanded. The most common designs now include the large Tekke *gul* which in Afghanistan is called the *akhel* gul, the *purdah* design, and the Zaher Shahi design. The Zaher Shahi was resuscitated by King Zaher Shah in the 1940s and is a simplified version of the *kedshebe gul* of the older Saruq design. (See Colour Plates 88 and 89).

The carpet bazaar in Herat is permanent, held in a small *serai* in the old city. There are also a number of dealers whose small shops — tourist traps — belie the amount of trade they handle; many of these shopkeepers are middlemen who operate from warehouses sending goods in bulk to Kabul. Herat is one of the major carpet-producing centres where natural dyes are extensively used in Turkoman goods, that is, the Mauris. The wool is Karaqul from Badghis Province to the north, where many Pashtun *maldars,* or animal owners, graze their large herds of sheep.

Ghorian is particularly famous for its typical prayer rug design (see Colour Plate 90), though in current production the camel hair field has been replaced by white wool. In addition, Mauri pieces of all sizes are made by the Tekkes here. Ghorian is also an important centre for various Beluch-type rugs.

Herat. A vertical loom, not traditional and never used except in the ateliers of Kabul and Herat. A relatively recent development.

Mauri Characteristics:

General: Firm, silky handle. Flat, tidy back; small, tight knotting. Single wefted, also *yak-o-neem tara,* literally 'one and a half strings', which means a normal weft plus a very fine weft. Also double wefted, usually in larger carpets. Both natural and synthetic dyes.

Designs: Small Tekke *gul, akhel gul,* Zaher Shahi design *purdah, narche gashtai,* and others. All Karaqul wool; white motifs of Kandahari wool. Plain white *kilim.*

Colours: Madder, red, indigo, brown made from walnut and pomegranate, white. Orange and green are also used.

Warps: 2-ply undyed Karaqul wool.

Wefts: 2-ply undyed Karaqul wool.

Selvedges: Blue, red, sometimes undyed; blanket stitch.

Knots: Asymmetric.

Sizes: All sizes, including prayer rugs.

Herat atelier

The Yamoud Carpet

In Afghanistan, the Yamoud Turkomans are found only in Herat, where, after settling, they began weaving their age-old designs brought from their homeland. However, these designs were not locally appreciated, so they took to copying the designs of the Tekkes and Saruqs, who had also settled in Herat. Today the rugs and carpets woven by the Yamouds which form part of the Mauri production, are indistinguishable from the pieces being woven by the Herat Tekkes and Saruqs. The materials, the weaving techniques and the dyes, as well as sizes and designs, are all similar. (See Colour Plate 91).

Yamoud Characteristics:

General: Firm, silky handle. Single wefted, but also *yak-o-neem tara,* literally 'one and a half strings', which means a normal weft plus a very fine weft. Double wefts usually in larger carpets. Both natural and synthetic dyes.

Designs: Small Tekke *gul, akhel gul,* Zaher Shahi design, *purdah, narche gashtai.* All Karaqul wool; white motifs of Kandahari wool. Plain white *kilim.*

Colours: Red, madder, indigo, white, gold.

Warps: 2-ply undyed Karaqul wool.

Wefts: 2-ply undyed brown Karaqul wool, or dyed red.

Selvedges: Blue, red, sometimes undyed; blanket stitch.

Knots: Asymmetric.

Sizes: All sizes, including prayer rugs.

The Saruq Carpet (Turkoman)

There are only about twenty Saruq families in Herat, not all of whom always weave the Saruq design. As already stated, the real home of this Turkoman tribe in Afghanistan is Marucharkh in Badghis Province. However, as the Saruq production is marketed in Herat, it is fitting that its description should appear here.

     The Saruq production is limited, probably not more than 600 to 800 square

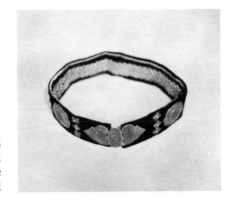

Yamoud Turkoman man's belt

88

90

Colour Plate 88 A MAURI rug depicting the Zaher Shahi design.

89

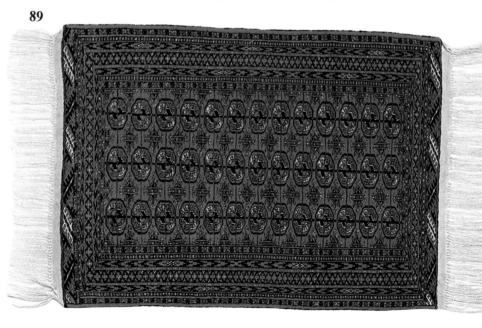

***Colour Plate 90** TEKKE Turkoman prayer rug from Ghorian. This very fine piece is dated 1332 (1953). Note the camel hair; more recent pieces contain white wool instead. (119 x 89cm).*
Courtesy of Alexander Gondris

***Colour Plate 89** MAURI yak-o-neem tara rug with Bokhara design. The curling corners is a frequent defect in these and yak tara (single wefted pieces), which is due to returning the weft too tightly at the end of a row of knots.*
Collection of Mrs. S.M. Parsons

91

92

Colour Plate 92 A SARUQ rug. (196 x 126cm).

Colour Plate 91 A typical modern YAMOUD KILIM from
Herat portraying the bastani motif. (242 x 122cm).

metres annually. They have maintained their fine quality of weave and their traditional designs of the large *gul* with a spiky border, which in the Soviet Union is referred to as the Salor *gul*. The Saruqs weave few large carpets, though their designs are reproduced in large sizes in the Andkhoy production. The ground colour is usually indigo, with two variations; an aubergine ground, obtained by mixing red with indigo, and sometimes a ground of natural camel hair. The similarity of the *guls* and colour combinations would suggest that it is a Salor product; however, there are no Salors in Afghanistan. (See Colour Plate 92).

Saruq Characteristics:

General: Firm, supple handle. Clean, narrowly ridged back; fine tight, regular knotting. Double wefted. Synthetic dyestuffs.

Designs: Traditional Saruq *gul* (sometimes referred to as Salor *gul),* all Karaqul wool. Plain white *kilims.*

Colours: Indigo, red and white, also aubergine and camel.

Warps: Usually 2-ply undyed Karaqul wool, though increasing use of white machine-spun blended yarn.

Wefts: Finely spun single-ply undyed Karaqul wool.

Selvedges: Indigo; blanket stitch.

Knots: Asymmetric.

Sizes: Mainly rug sizes.

Chapter 12
The Afghan Beluch Rug

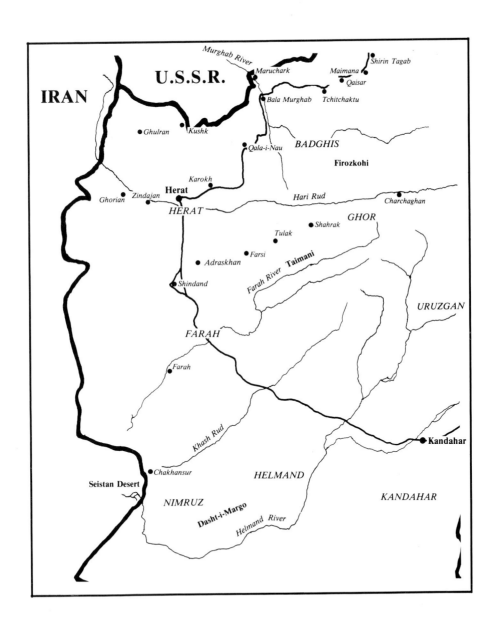

Although there are nomadic Beluch throughout Afghanistan, they do not, by any means, all make carpets and rugs. The two main production centres of the

93a

Colour Plate 93a A section of an old BELUCH-TYPE carpet from southwest Afghanistan made in three strips. An interesting piece insofar as the design is intricate and the kilims unusually long, measuring 41 and 38cm, and which by colour and design undoubtedly signify Pashtu-speaking semi-nomads. The weave is loose and the yarn fairly coarse, suggesting a Ghormaj-Taimani influence, but probably made by the Mushwanis of southwest Afghanistan. (287 x 160cm).

Shir Khosrow Paiwand

93

Colour Plate 93 A typical BELUCH KILIM woven in one piece. (340 x 165cm).

Author's collection

93b

93c

Colour Plate 93b A classical CHAKHANSUR BELUCH rug. This delightful piece displays all the qualities associated with the renowned Chakhansur-Beluch production, an area from which come the real Beluch rugs as opposed to the Beluch-type. These attributes include fine hand-spun yarn, fine and tight knotting, the use of natural dyestuffs in conjunction with undyed brown yarn and large distinctive kilims. The construction makes for a light yet firm handle. The design depicted is fairly common. The kilims measure 18cm each. (168 x 109cm).

Shir Khosrow Paiwand

Colour Plate 93c An antique Beluch prayer rug, probably from SANG CHULI, a village to the south-west of Gulran in Badghis Province. Of fine weave and in good condition, this piece is dated 1261 AH (1882). In common with a number of rugs made at the turn of the century, this piece has silk motifs. These appear throughout the rug, but are especially evident in the leaves of the flower vase just below the date; also in the line bisecting the stylised leaves of the field. Note the two double rams' horns — essentially a Turkoman motif — at the bottom of the panel. (140 x 107cm).

Shir Khosrow Paiwand

Afghan Beluch are Chakhansur district which lies in the irrigated part of the Seistan desert and the area west and south-west of Herat city which adjoins the Iranian frontier. The goods from the latter are referred to as 'Sarhadis' (Sarhad means frontier or boundary in Dari).

Common features of both the Chakhansur and Sarhadi production, much of which is woven by the largely sedentary Rukhshani Beluch are the quality of weave and the colours. Fineness of stitch and tightness of weave are characteristic, as is the generally sombre colouring, with its harmonious interplay of hues. Indigo, various shades of blue and red are the preferred colours; however, the variety of both designs and colours increases each year. The soft and well-sorted wool, from either the Beluchi or Ghilzai breeds of sheep, readily develops a natural sheen after comparatively little use, and the traditional dyestuffs used oxidise fairly rapidly, resulting in mellow tones. (See Colour Plate 93).

Some of these goods, particularly the Sarhadis, are taken across the border to Iran where they are often sold for a higher price than would be obtained in Herat.

One distinct type of Sarhadi is woven by the Zurhuri tribe, whose name is derived from the Zurhur Mountains not far from Farah. The Zurhuris, who are said to be of Arab descent and, therefore, not Beluch, began making rugs of a new design a few years ago. In about 1976, these goods started to appear in ever-increasing numbers. The simple design displays a reddy-maroon medallion set in a cream field. (See Colour Plate 94).

The production from Farah, which lies due north of Chakhansur and borders the Sarhadi area to the east, falls within a grey zone. The majority of the population is Pashtun, with some semi-sedentary Beluch.

The Farah rug resembles that of the Beluch, from whom the Pashtun in the area learned to weave. The production is not large, and the goods are not so fine as the true Beluch weave from either Chakhansur or the Sarhadi area. The colours are nearly always sombre, and the carpets are usually long and narrow.

Farah used to be noted for its *kilims,* and some are still obtainable in the market. They were finely woven, with predominant colours of dark blue and deep maroon red, sometimes a very dark green, and seldom any white. Present-day production of *kilims* is rather coarse and the designs are plainer, being merely a series of coloured lateral bands.

Another centre, whose production is difficult to place absolutely in either the Beluch or the Beluch-type category, is Adraskhan, due north of Farah on the Kandahar-Herat road, some seventy kilometres south of Herat. The production from this area is considerable and appears to be increasing, especially the carpet sizes and large rugs. The local tribes are predominantly Alizai and Nurzai — both Pashtun — who learned the craft from the Beluch. As would be expected in such a large production, there is a wide variance in quality, with the best pieces being very fine indeed. The Adraskhan rug as a whole tends to be thick with a fairly long pile. Colouring is generally rather dark, deep purples, indigo, green and deep brown. The traditional geometric diamond design, with nearly always a white motif in each corner of the field, is easily recognisable. (See Colour Plate 95).

Kilims, very similar to those of Farah, used to be made in the Adrakhshan district, but this industry has greatly declined and what is produced today tends to be coarse and less intricate.

The Afghan Beluch and Beluch-type Production

The Beluch production in Afghanistan is limited. By far the majority of goods fall into the Beluch-type category. Geographically, the two areas are

Chaparis

94a

Colour Plate 94a *Section of a CHAKHANSUR carpet depicting the classical and familiar* kalam donneh *(pencil box) design. While small sizes were made and are still to be found, the larger sizes are more common, usually long and narrow and often up to 3-3.6m in length. The section shown is approximately half the total length, there being five rows each having three* kalam donneh *motifs. The upper kilim measures 25cm, the lower 22cm. (Circa 1910; 342 x 196cm).*

In olden times, the Beluch from Chakhansur would seasonally migrate north and pieces such as this one could be found in the Gulran district of Badghis Province.

Shir Khosrow Paiwand

95a

95b

Colour Plate 95a *An old FARAH carpet made in two pieces. Although depicting the* owzi* *design which is associated with the Adraskhan production (see Colour Plate 95), the back of this carpet has a much rougher feel than comparable Adraskhan pieces, denoting the use of somewhat overspun yard, a characteristic of the Farah production, which also gives the back a different appearance. A peculiar feature of this piece is its shape, which is almost square. The kilims are wide, the upper measuring 33cm and the lower 31cm. (Late 19th century; 215 x 191cm).*

Shir Khosrow Paiwand

* In Dari, the Persian word *ab* (water) is pronounced *ow*. Thus the *owzi* design can be translated as the 'water-like' or 'pool' design.

Colour Plate 95b *An old Beluch rug from FARAH. Note the kilims, each of which measures 25cm and which are typical in colouring and design of the semi-nomadic Pashtu-speaking tribes of this area producing Beluch-type goods. Also typical of the 'S' motif at both ends. Whilst the* boteh *motif is common in the rug production of this area, it is unusual to find an 'all-over'* boteh *pattern. The fineness and originality of this rug, dating from circa 1930, suggest a dowry piece. (130 x 105cm).*

Shir Khosrow Paiwand

94

95

Colour Plate 94 A ZURHURI *rug. (167 x 97cm). The production from Farah, which lies due north of Chakhansur and borders the Sarhadi area to the east, falls within a grey zone. The majority of the population is Pashtun, with some semi-sedentary Beluch.*

Colour Plate 95 An ADRASKHAN *Beluch-type rug. The design, especially the white motif in each corner, and the sombre colouring, are very typical. In this production the pile tends to be long, and the yarn is soft, which result in a good sheen after comparatively little usage. Other features of this production are the fine weave and dense texture of the fabric. (223 x 135cm).*

96a

Colour Plate 96a *An old TAIMANI
rug from the Ghor region of west
central Afghanistan. This
harmonious piece, dating from circa
1935, has a classical weaving
structure and the colours that are
found in the older Charchaghan
kilims, i.e., madder, a soft olive
green, indigo, gold and undyed
brown wool. The upper kilim
measures 18cm, the lower 14cm.
(161 x 111cm).*

Shir Khosrow Paiwand

approximately equal in size, but the population of the northern area producing the Beluch-type goods is infinitely greater than that of the southern desert regions.

Of the Beluch-type production a substantial quantity is made by four tribes called the 'Chahar Aimaq'. Aimaq as used here is a Mongolian word meaning nomad. These four tribes are basically semi-nomadic, of mixed origin, and are all Persian speaking.

Of the Chahar Aimaq, the largest group is undoubtedly the Taimani, of whom there are at least ten main divisions and numerous sub-clans. Taimani country is the mountainous area to the south east of Herat, and south of the Hari Rud river, which is the boundary dividing them from the Firozkohi, another Chahar Aimaq tribe. Scenically, Taimani country is very striking. In the upper reaches of the Hari Rud, after following a tortuous track along a narrow valley bounded on either side by high craggy mountains, rises the awe-inspiring twelfth-century Minaret of Jam in solitary splendour. Discovered only in 1957, it is, at two hundred and thirteen feet, the second tallest minaret in the world and a most magnificent example of Islamic architecture. It is thought to mark the capital of the ancient Ghorid dynasty, although the mystery surrounding this isolated monument is still unsolved.

Nomads on the move

The Taimani and their Production

The Taimani are semi-nomadic, that is to say, people who own land which they cultivate but who live in tents for most of the year while they herd their flocks in search of grazing. In winter they return to their permanent quarters.

The Taimani carpet production is quite varied. In the southern part of the region, around the towns of Tulak and Farsi, there is a very large production of Taimani goods — mostly prayer rugs — which is marketed in Shindand. (See Colour Plate 96). Shindand is an important marketing centre for Beluch-type rugs made by the Taimani and also by the Nurzai, a Pashtun clan numerous in the area who have only recently taken up weaving. Shindand is also notable for the fact that it holds two carpet bazaars on its Thursday and Monday market days. When one bazaar ends at about 9.30 a.m., another takes over the business at the other end of the street and continues until noon.

The Shindand production varies considerably in quality and also in its design. Of these, a common one is the *seh mihrabha* or the three mihrabs; another well-known design is the *Dokhtar-i-Qazi* or the Judge's Daughter, said to be so named because it was first created and woven by for a local Qazi's daughter. (See Colour Plates 97 and 98).

Another type of rug woven by Taimanis, marketed in Shindand, comes from the district of Sakhar, near the town of Farsi. This Sakhari rug has a coarse weave, and its design is a simple *mihrab* and a field containing a repetitive motif which is often a parallelogram. These pieces almost invariably contain orange and white. Other designs are a copy of either the *kar-i-sefide* or the *Yaqub Khanah* (House of Jacob, after the Yaqub Khanah sub-tribe). In the London market, this design is also called the *Yaqub Khani* (of Yaqub Khan) suggesting that this design was that of the followers of the warrior Yaqub Khan, who now form the Yaqub Khanah sub-tribe.

The provincial capital of Ghor Province is Charchaghan which has given its name to the Charchaghan *kilim,* also made by the Taimani.

This sturdy yet finely woven fabric has bands of intricate designs in soft colours which include purple, green, gold and red. The new production tends to be dominated by a strong purple, sometimes also by orange, and often the bands of designs are more widely spaced. The texture, however, is good and strong, and the Charchaghan *kilim* makes a good, hard-wearing and heavy

146

Colour Plate 96 TAIMANI *prayer rug from the Ghor region — a very typical example of today's production. (144 x 91cm).*

Colour Plate 97 SEH MIHRABHA (three *mihrabs) prayer rug. A typical example of the better pieces marketed in Shandand. Note the 'star' motif so often seen in the Taimani production, and also copied and incorporated by the transhumants who cross Taimani country during migrations.*

Colour Plate 98 DOKHTARI-I-QAZI *prayer rug (Shindand production). (133 x 88cm).*

Collection Mark Parsons, Esq.

98a

Colour Plate 98a A DOKHTAR-I-QAZI prayer rug. Although this piece was woven in the Shindand district of southwest Afghanistan, there is an unmistakable Chakhansur influence, vide the colours and striped design of the kilims, as well as their length (the lower one measuring 12cm, the upper 9cm). In addition, the use of madder and indigo with white wool is a typical feature of this production. A delightful piece dating from circa 1910. (148 x 101cm).

Shir Khosrow Paiwand

99

Colour Plate 99 CHARCHAGHAN KILIM. *This type of* kilim *is amongst the finest and most durable of the* Afghan kilims. *The floating weft technique is used in its construction. (341 x 207cm).*

floor covering which does not ruckle. Sizes vary from just over 3m², to 9m², the larger pieces tending to be long and narrow. (See Colour Plate 99).

Taimanis do not own large flocks of sheep. much of the wool used in their production comes from the Ghilzai sheep owned by Pashtun *maldars* who graze their herds in the Ghorid mountains during the summer. The dyes used by the Taimani are now virtually all synthetic.

The Firozkohi and Their Production

Chaparis

The Firozkohi (Mountain of Turquoise), who live in the area east of the Qala-i-Nau Hazara and north of the Taimani, are another Chahar Aimaq tribe. They are mainly semi-nomadic, living in small *yurt*-like tents called *chaparis.* The tribe can be roughly divided into two main groups, each having numerous sub-clans. Those living in the eastern part are more Mongolian in feature than the large Mahmud group of the west.

Their production of rugs is varied, and on the whole the quality is average. Having no designs of their own, they copy known designs and, like the Taimani, they favour purple and orange. Dyes are all synthetic.

However, their production of flat-woven goods is more distinctive. They make *torbahs,* and many of the most popular *namak donnehs* (salt bags) are made by the Firozkohis. They weave *kilims* and *khourjeens.* (See Colour Plate 100). Frequently they embroider a flimsy, flat-woven cloth of natural dark brown wool with wool of several colours in concentric diamond motifs. Orange, pale green, white and cherry red are common colour combinations for these *dasterkhans,* or eating cloths. (The term *dasterkhan* also refers to the family — the family all eat off the eating cloth).

They also make saddle cloths and horse blankets for their own use. In the north, Karaqul wool is used; Ghilzai wool in the south.

The Jamshidi and Their Production

The Jamshidi, another tribe of the Chahar Aimaq, are dispersed through Badghis and Herat provinces where many are semi-nomadic. There is also a fairly large colony of sedentary Jamshidi living in Herat city. The origin of the Jamshidi is obscure. Some claim to be of Arab stock, others to have originated from Persia. The Jamshidi, over the years, have had considerable contact with Turkomans. This may well be the reason that their production so much resembles that of the Tekkes of Herat. Having no designs of their own, the Jamshidi copy the Mauri designs; the Zaher Shahi design is also quite often seen. Jamshidi goods are frequently sold as Mauris.

There are differences, however, and weave is one of them. With a few exceptions, it can be said that the Jamshidi production is of a looser construction. In addition, the stitches are coarser and squarer. Much of the Jamshidi pieces are of *yak-o-neem tara* ('one and a half strings'), meaning that alternate wefts are of different thickness. The Jamshidi only make rug sizes, i.e. sizes up to 200 x 150cm. Wool is Karaqul, as they are here in Karaqul country, and dyes are synthetic.

The Kawdani Prayer Rug

The Kawdani are a very small clan, believed to be an offshoot of the Jamshidi. They live in the village of Jaffa Beg which is not far from Kushk in the north of Herat Province.

100

101

Colour Plate 101 KAWDANI prayer rug. This piece depicts a stylised Tree of Life, a design frequently used in this production, which is among the finest of the Afghan Beluch-type. The selvedges are of goat hair. (141 x 89cm).
Author's collection

Colour Plate 100 A FIROZKOHI KILIM. The embroidery is in wool. (268 x 131cm).

102/103

104

Colour Plate 102 *A LAGHARI KILIM, typical of those made by the Suni Hazaras who live in and around Qala-i-Nau. These pieces, always woven in two strips and then joined, are easily identified by their colourful designs which consist of narrow bands of simple repetitive motifs in which the influence of both the Taimani Charchaghan and also the Beluch is discernible. Cherry red is a preferred colour which often dominates this production. (258 x 192cm).*

Colour Plate 103 *Semi-antique SHIRKHANI prayer rug with natural undyed wool ground depicting animals and birds. The strict Muslim does not allow representations of either human or animal form in decorative art. Thus it is safe to assume that such pieces were made in places far from the influence of mullahs. In this piece, the stylised figures are reminiscent of the Afsharis from Iran. A skeletal stylised Tree of Life, so often portrayed in Shirkhani rugs is discernible in this piece.*

Colour Plate 104 *A JAN BEGI rug. (196 x 130cm).*

Like the Jamshidi, they are Persian speaking and also weave rugs of very fine quality. Their production is small, always double wefted, and consists almost entirely of prayer rugs, with a Tree of Life design. Camel hair nearly always appears in the ground and very often in a border guard as well. The blues are usually indigo and the reds are synthetic dyestuffs. They do not make carpet sizes. (See Colour Plate 101).

The Qala-i-Nau Hazara and Their Production

The fourth member of the Chahar Aimaq tribes is the Qala-i-Nau Hazara, who live in and around the small town of Qala-i-Nau, the capital of Badghis Province. This tribe of Hazara are Sunni Muslims referred to as Sunni Hazaras, quite different from the Hazara native to the Hazarajat region of central Afghanistan who are Shi'a Muslims. As with the Hazara of the Hazarajat they are said to be descendants of the hordes who accompanied Genghis Khan. However, another theory claims they only settled here in the middle of the eighteenth century when they were forcibly displaced from the Hazarajat by King Nadir Shah.

Sunni Hazaras were traditionally known for their fine *kilims*. They have more or less abandoned this craft except for the very limited production from Laghari, a small village near Qala-i-Nau. The attractive Laghari *kilim* is easily recognised by rather narrow adjoining bands of intricate designs in which a predominant cherry red contrasts strikingly with the other colours of subdued tone. At each end there is a band about twenty-five centimetres wide of dark brown natural wool, often decorated by one or more barber pole motifs. The Laghari *kilim* is fairly small, seldom exceeding 4m² and frequently woven on a narrow loom in two strips sewn up the middle. (See Colour Plate 102).

In about 1972, the Sunni Hazaras of Qala-i-Nau began to produce both rugs and carpets of good quality, which are difficult to distinguish from the Jamshidi production, as techniques, designs and colouring are similar. More recently still, these Sunni Hazaras started to weave a stylised *purdah* design similar to that of Qaisar (see page 127) another interesting change in the Afghan carpet industry. Karaqul wool is used and dyes are synthetic.

The remaining production of Beluch-type carpets and rugs of any significance comes from various regions of Herat and Badghis provinces. As already mentioned, it is difficult to identify places and production with complete accuracy, since many weavers are semi-nomadic; they are great copiers and often place and tribal names are duplicated. Furthermore, a single place can have as many as five different names, depending on whether you ask a Pashtun, a Farsi speaker, a local permanent inhabitant, a nomad passing through or a government official from Kabul! Confusion also arises from the similarity of clan names of totally different ethnic groups. For instance the Alizais are recognised as a major division of the Pashtun Durrani tribe but there is also a Jamshidi sub-clan called Alizai.

The following better-known Beluch-type rugs and carpets are given by tribal identification and geographic area. In general, the wool used is that of the breed of sheep predominant in the area, with Badghis and north Herat provinces being Karaqul country and Herati, Gaadic and Ghilzai sheep found further south. Dyestuffs are today virtually all synthetic.

The Shirkhani Rug

The Shirkhani is another semi-nomadic Persian-speaking tribe, believed to be of Alizai Pashtun origin, living in the Zindajan district of the Hari Rud river some forty-five kilometres west of Herat. The main design of this typical Beluch-type rug is the Tree of Life, which could be mistaken for the Kawdani prayer rug, though it is not so fine. (See Colour Plate 103).

The Jan Begi Rug

The Jan Begi are a very small Persian-speaking tribe who are mostly found in the Ghorian district and Kusan, a district comprising some twenty-five villages about fifty kilometres north-west of Ghorian. The authentic Jan Begi carpet is small and of excellent quality. Today their well-known repetitive floral motif is being widely copied, notably in some of the Tchitchaktu production in sun-faded tones.

From Herat city an increasing number of carpets bearing the Jan Begi floral motif, woven by all and sundry, are appearing on the market. However, the traditional Jan Begi red is often replaced by a cream or beige in this Herat production. (See Colour Plate 104).

The Haft Bolah Rug

The Haft Bolah, or Seven Demons, are a small Pashtu-speaking tribe which, like the Jan Begi, are to be found in Ghorian and the Kusan district of Herat Province. The Haft Bolah rug has an unmistakable series of narrow border guards which appear in all their prayer rugs and rugs. The latter range in sizes from 2m² to 3m² (200 x 100 to 225 x 150cm). The tightly tied knot is rather square and the quality is good. Two fairly common faults in this production are the tendency to clip the pile too low and also many pieces are often crooked. (See Colour Plate 105).

The Mandali Production

The Persian-speaking tribe of Mandali lives around the district of Karokh, some forty kilometres north of Herat. They are known for their large production of coarse rugs. Like many other tribes mentioned in this section, they have no designs of their own. The designs which they copy are many and varied, and change periodically. For some years the Mandali had a penchant for weaving Turkoman designs, especially the 'elephant foot' octagon. They also make a few carpet sizes and these are nearly always long and narrow.

The Mushwani Rug

The Mushwani are of Pashtun origin, but many of those who live in Afghanistan are now Persian-speaking. This tribe, which is widely dispersed in both Badghis and Herat provinces, is both sedentary and semi-nomadic. The former which are concentrated around Gulran and Qala-i-Nau were famed for their very fine *kilims,* the borders and part of the field of which were elaborately embroidered. Always of sombre colours, these *kilims* were amongst the finest made in Afghanistan. Those made especially for dowries were veritable works of art. Some fifteen or so years ago, the Mushwani totally abandoned *kilim* weaving and instead began to make rugs. Their production today is both substantial and of good quality.

Further south, around Karokh, there are some nomadic Mushwani who also weave rugs, many of which are of the same design as those described.

Painted lorry, typically Pashtun

105 **106**

Colour Plate 105 HAFT BOLAH *(literally 'seven up')*
prayer rug. Apart from the regular squarish knot, it is the
border guards, as shown in this photograph, which are so
typical and as such make recognition of this quality easy.
The best examples of the Haft Bolah production are made
in rug sizes rather than prayer rug formats. (152 x 97cm).

Colour Plate 106 MUSHWANI *rug. Prayer rugs are perhaps*
more common than rugs. The main distinguishing features
of this production are the repetitive mihrabs all around the
field and the pronounced incidence of old gold. (170 x
91cm).

Colour Plate 107 MUSHWANI *prayer rug. (142 x 85cm).*

107

Colour Plate 108 YAQUB KHANI *rug. This design is frequently reproduced in carpet sizes. The design form tends to accentuate pieces which are already long and narrow, a feature of so many Beluch and Beluch-type carpets. Like the Dokhtar-i-Qazi, the Yaqub Khani generally comprises only red and blue, although sometimes white does appear in the designs. (165 x 96cm).*

Colour Plate 109 Oldish GHORMAJ *mat. Typical of this production are: (i) coarse and rather loose weave. (ii) simple and uncrowded geometric designs. (iii) a tendency to use purple and orange. (iv) double fringes, as depicted at one end of the piece illustrated. Prayer rugs are common. Sizes very seldom exceed 3.5m². (84 x 67cm).*

Mushwani rugs are unmistakable because of their unique broad border design. (See Colour Plates 106 and 107).

The Mushwanis also make a long and narrow *dasterkhan* (eating cloth) measuring about 200 x 60cm. This is a flat-woven rather flimsy fabric entirely covered with multicoloured embroidery or artificial silk.

Those Mushwanis in the south and west of Afghanistan who still make rugs are concentrated in an area from Shindand to Adraskhan. The designs are varied — with frequent use of the *seh mihrabha* (three mihrabs) — but rarely, if ever, do they execute the border shown in Colour Plates 106 and 107. The quality of their production is poorer than that of the Mushwanis who live to the north of Herat and in Badghis Province and is often of a cheap and dry yarn. They also tend to make rather dark and gloomy kilims of all sizes, which often have a purplish-brown field with coloured lateral stripes of varying widths.

The Yaqub Khanah Rug

The Yaqub Khanah (House of Jacob) is a small semi-nomadic Persian-speaking tribe. Some people believe them to be an offshoot of the Timuris, a tribe now mainly settled in Iran. The Yaqub Khanah tribe are found in and around Chulran, a town in the north-west of Herat Province. Their small production is of good quality and their well-known and popular design of elongated panels against an indigo field is being widely copied by other tribes. (See Colour Plate 108).

The Ishaqzais Production

The nomadic Ishaqzais, a segment of the large tribe of Pashtun Durranis, are to be found in various areas of the west and north-west of Afghanistan, and are particularly numerous around Ghulran in the north-west of Herat Province. They weave rugs of medium quality, and having no motifs of their own, a large range of run-of-the-mill designs. Their production is limited.

The Town of the Ghormaj and Its Production

Ghormaj, a small two-street town some thirty kilometres west of Tchitchaktu has given its name to the Ghormaj rug, often erroneously called the Taimani. The reason for this misnomer is not clear; the local population is made up of Durrani Pashtuns, some Uzbeks and a few Aimaqs — but virtually no Taimani. Perhaps the confusion arises because the Taimanis live in the province of Ghor (Ghor equalling Ghormaj) or perhaps because the Ghormaj rug resembles the Taimani weave. This so-called Ghormaj rug has all but disappeared from the market.

The Ghormaj rug was coarsely constructed, with simple rustic designs, making it one of the most 'tribal' looking rugs woven in Afghanistan. Many were prayer rugs, usually less than 1m² and rather squarish in shape. A common feature of these pieces was the wide *kilim* at both ends, sometimes with double fringes, often simply yet effectively decorated. Rugs having a cross-latch design and seldom exceeding 3m² (200 x 125cm) were also made; these pieces quite frequently contained camel-coloured wool. Whilst some of these can still be found on the local market, they are becoming increasingly rare for the simple reason that they are no longer being made. Instead, the weavers of these goods have turned their hands to making the 'Tchitchaktu' type of rug. This production from Ghormaj is the poorest of the Tchitchaktu being made, and is mostly sold in Qaisar. Thus, we see here another example of these changes taking place in the Afghan carpet scene; the disappearance of one type of rug, replaced by a totally different product, of poor quality. (See Colour Plate 109).

Pashtun shepherd

In and around Ghormaj are made Beluch-type *boleshts,* or pillow bags, measuring about 90 x 60cm with an opening at the narrow end. *Khourjeens* and a few rather coarse *kilims* are also made here, but in spite of this, Ghormaj does not rank as a carpet-producing area. Neither is there a carpet bazaar as such. This two-street town boasts no more than three shops dealing in woven goods, and these are largely cotton *sadranjis* and Hazaragi *kilims* brought in by itinerant traders.

The Tchitchaktu Production

This distinctive Beluch-type rug was unknown before the summer of 1971 when it first began to appear on the market. It is yet another typical example of the constant change taking place in the Afghan carpet scene.

The term 'Tchitchaktu' may cause some raised eyebrows, for these carpets are not generally known by this name abroad. It seems logical, however, to call them after the bazaar from where they are sold, in the area where they are made.

Tchitchaktu is a small and picturesque two-street town on the northern Circular Route some ninety kilometres south-west of Maimana. It is a market town serving a community of diverse tribes consisting mainly of Pashtun, Uzbek, Aimaq and some Tajik. The Pashtun are not native to this area, having been forcibly settled here by King Abdurahman in the late 1880s, in his largely successful attempts to subjugate the many warring tribes and establish a central government from Kabul. The Pashtun learned the craft of weaving from those Uzbek and Aimaq of the region who made such domestic necessities as *kilims, khourjeens* and *boleshts* — but not carpets. It was but a short step to the making of prayer rugs. There is only a handful of Turkomans living in the town itself; they do not, however, weave any of their traditional products, except for a few *khourjeens* and *kilims.*

There are several Pashtun sub-tribes who now produce the Tchitchaktu. Of these, the Durrani, who originate from Kandahar, are perhaps the most skilful and prolific weavers.

The quality of the Tchitchaktu rug varies considerably, and it is impossible to attribute any one piece to any particular tribe. It success was so marked and production increased so rapidly that by 1077, the main street could no longer contain the carpet bazaar and it moved to its separate area south of the central street.

The reasons for the sudden upsurge of weaving in an area with practically no carpet making traditions are twofold. Firstly, due to the catastrophic droughts of 1971 and 1972, the sheep of this region — as others — were decimated. Mounting stocks of 'dead' wool salvaged from the starved carcasses and the shearing of dying sheep assured a source of raw material which the local people, seeking an income, were forced to put to the most profitable use. They turned to weaving, which craft they learned from neighbouring Turkomans. Secondly, the carpet boom of 1972 and 1973 when both prices and demand shot up, could not have been more opportune; rug making as a local industry was established.

During the tragic period of the drought, the quality of wool in carpets from most areas obviously declined, because of the use of 'dead' wool. Many finely woven Mauris from those years, for instance, will not last as long as a carpet of the same workmanship woven with healthy wool. This, however, was temporary and generally speaking, it is only in the very cheap qualities, especially in Qarqeens and lowest grades of Kizilayak and Aq Chah goods that 'dead' wool is used today. The tradition of a good craftsman using good material is being maintained throughout Afghanistan. The except to this rule is due to ignorance or commercial greed.

108a

Colour Plate 108a. A very striking and unusual YAQUB KHANI rug. The highlighting of three central panels in white immediately catches the eye and possibly hinders immediate identification. In addition, the panels are smaller than those in current production. This piece, which dates from circa 1930, is excellently preserved. (213 x 113cm).

110

111

Colour Plate 110 A TCHITCHAKTU rug with the panj mihrabha *(five* mihrabs) *design. (140 x 93cm).*
Collection Mrs. S.M. Parsons

Colour Plate 111 TCHITCHAKTU mat depicting a stylised purdah design. These small sizes were rarely seen prior to the spring of 1978. (74 x 58cm).
Author's collection

The origin of the Tchitchaktu design is less clear. Various sources claim that a foreign buyer commissioned this design from a photograph through a Pashtun *mullah* of the area. If this is true, then presumably either the design was transcribed on graph paper, or else a number of prototypes were made and passed around for copying.

When production of the Tchitchaktu first began, practically the only design used was the *panj mihrabha,* the name under which many of these pieces are marketed. The *mihrab* is that niche in every mosque throughout the world that always points to Mecca. Although called five *mihrabs,* in fact, the design can contain any number of niches, between five and seventeen. (See Colour Plate 110).

Gradually, other designs, such as copies of the Jan Begi, Zaher Shahi, etc., were introduced, and during 1978, a bastardised form of the *purdah* or *hatchlu,* became very popular, as did stylised birds found in Caucasian rugs. (See Colour Plate 111). A superior quality of the Tchitchaktu rug is also woven by non-Turkoman families in Sharkh, some thirty kilometres to the sout-west.

Surprisingly, and simultaneously with the development of the Tchitchaktu production, began the practice of 'ageing' the goods, using a primitive, yet effective form of chemical washing. Quicklime mixed with ashes and formed into a paste is smeared over the rug. After drying in the sun, the rug is washed and the pile is combed with an object resembling a horse scraper. The resulting mellowness of colours, especially of reds, is very pleasing. Indigo is always used and because the blue is not affected by the bleaching process, those pieces successfully treated have an appeal that immediately catches the eye. The blues contrast strikingly with the soft rusty browns, fawns and creams.

Not infrequently, the bleaching is overdone and this is particularly evident in the poorer quality pieces which end up looking and feeling like a well-used dishcloth.

Although the general appearance of the Tchitchaktu is very attractive — good design, good colour, a size which renders it suitable for wall hangings as well as floor coverings — all too often the structure of the piece has been damaged by the methods used in the 'ageing'. As a result, the wool loses much of its wearing properties, and given the slightest twist, the warps will snap. Often these pieces have a damaged *kilim* and fringes, also due to the adverse effects of the quicklime.

Tchitchaktu Characteristics

General: Handle varies; in the better qualities, a supple velvety feel, the poorer pieces empty, floppy handle, back variable; squarish knotting. Double wefted, synthetic dyes.

Design: Five *mihrabs,* stylised *purdah* Jan Begi, Zaher Shahi, and others; all Karaqul wool. Plain *kilim.*

Colours: Indigo, red, brown, fawn, cream.

Warps: 2-ply undyed Karaqul wool.

Wefts: 2-ply undyed Karaqul wool.

Selvedges: Undyed Karaqul wool; blanket stitch.

Knots: Asymmetric.

Sizes: Average size 1.20^2, rarely exceeds $1.50m^2$ (120 x 100, 135 x 115cm).

Chapter 13
The Hazara Kilim

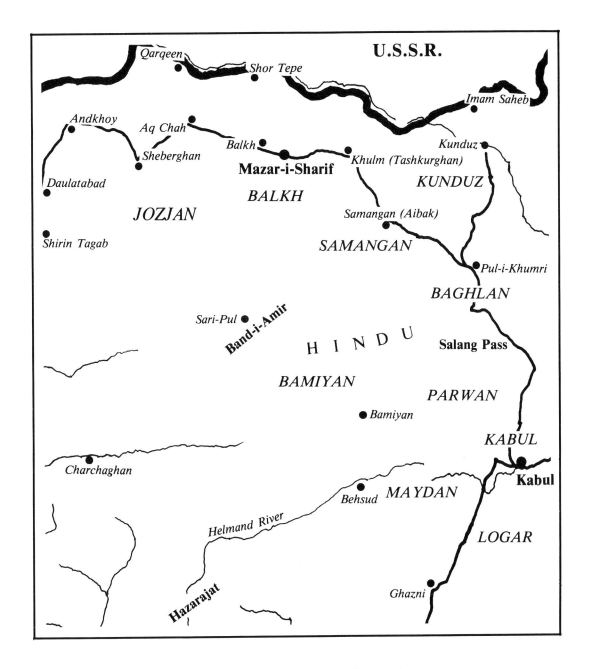

The Hazara people, who inhabit the vast mountainous area of central
Afghanistan, are quite different from the other ethnic groups of this

Hindu Kush

Terrace cultivation

The central mountains of the Hazarajat

Hindu Kush in winter

multiracial country. Their hardy, stocky frames and round, nearly hairless faces are evidence of their Mongolian origins. The Hazara are traditionally believed to be descended from Mongol Tartar regiments brought into this region by Genghis Khan but they certainly originate from Chinese Turkestan. The lack of arable land in the austere region of the mountains of the Hazarajat has forced many Hazaras to seek work in the towns, as domestic servants in hotels and private homes, or as porters and building labourers. Those who remain eke out a living on the narrow strips of land, often terraced, in the small valleys scattered through the craggy, inhospitable ranges of the Hindu Kush.

Although poor, many desperately so, the Hazaras are extremely hospitable and a traveller is always sure of being offered food and shelter. He will sleep in a mosque, also used as the *mehman khana,* literally 'guest room', which is the pivotal point of even the poorest hamlet, and be given a thin cotton-filled palliasse spread out on the floor and a quilted cotton blanket for the night. The food may be nothing more than dry bread and tea in the morning and at night some greasy soup in which as much bread as possible is soaked, but after a hard journey, such amenities are indeed welcome and appreciated. The traveller soon falls asleep and all too soon is awakened by the murmur of the devout who have come to recite their early morning prayers. In winter, when the deep layers of snow make work and travel impossible, the men gather in the mosque to gossip, to listen to stories and recitations from the Koran. The room is kept warm by the heat from a dung and brushwood fire, which circulates in specially constructed channels under the floor.

The Hazara are essentially farmers, and their poverty precludes their owning large numbers of domestic animals. In the *woleswali* of Jaghuri, some fifty kilometres west of Behsud, where the mountains are exceptionally steep and jagged, the entire flock of sheep of a village may number only sixty or seventy animals. Here it is rare for any one man to own more than ten animals, whereas in the Behsud area, a rich man, of which there are not many, may own up to fifty sheep. For eight months of the year, a shepherd boy will collect his charges at dawn to take them up the mountain sides to graze, and return them to their owners at dusk. He is paid in kind: usually ½ *seer* (3½ kilos) of corn per animal, which he receives at harvest time. In addition, he is fed and sometimes lodged by the sheep owners, following a complex, yet equitable, rota system. At autumn shearing, he further receives a customary gift of two ounces of wool per sheep from each owner.

This wool (called *shaali,* from the Persian *shal,* whence our 'shawl') is, by custom, made in a heavy outer garment or a pair of breeches, and is treated in rather a special way. After being hand-carded, spun and woven, the cloth is placed on the slab of stone over the fire that heats the mosque, where it is dampened and then trampled on with great vigour. When one person tires, another takes his place. This process continues, sometimes up to two days, until the material has shrunk and become somewhat 'felted', making it partly waterproof and certainly windproof.

An utter stillness and impersonal beauty overlie these vast land masses. The sparse vegetation and muted colours of earth and stone make a striking background for the bright green and gold patches of the tiny meadows and fields surrounding a village or hamlet. The essential character of the Hindu Kush is space and silence; they dominate this arid, infertile land which is a constant and continuous challenge to mankind. It is no wonder that the inhabitants of this region have developed a physical and spiritual attitude towards life that is both fatalistically stoic and serene.

Today, the Hazara are ardent Muslims of the Shi'a sect. A millenium and a half ago these valleys were devoutly Buddhist and rang with the chanting prayer of monks and pilgrims, as witnessed by the complex of stupas, monastic dwellings and gigantic Buddhas carved out of the cliff face of the

112

Colour Plate 112 *HAZARA KILIM from Sari-Pul. Although orange does not feature in this piece, it is nonetheless a good example of a typical Sari-Pul kilim. Both the design and construction are very typical, as is the* lab-i-Mazar *border motif. (189 x 126cm).*

Bamiyan valley

Weaving kilims (Hazara)

Tent pegging

Bamiyan Valley. In this extraordinary oasis, with its neatly cultivated fields, every square foot of soil is put to use, and in spring and summer, a rich scent of clover and wild mustard interspersed among plots of corn and lucerne, rises from the fertile earth. This valley has been much photographed and often described, as have the vivid blue lakes of Band-i-Amir, some seventy-five kilometres to the west, lying like huge irregular medallions of lapis-lazuli set in a tawny desert landscape.

The sheep native to the Hazarajat is the Hazaragi breed, also a fat-tail species, but the tail does not grow as large as that of the Arabi or Ghilzai. The wool, in a variety of colours, is soft and quite suitable for the making of cloth. It is also used for weaving domestic *kilims,* which do not appear in large numbers on the market. The designs of these are often merely bands of white and black or brown undyed wool. Sometimes a thick band of dyed wool (purple and wine red are favoured colours) is added for variation. Although made of soft wool, the wefts are beaten down so tightly during weaving that the *kilim* is tough and hard-wearing.

At the same time, there was a small production of commercial *kilims,* made with wool bought from passing nomads with their flocks of Ghilzai sheep. For a number of years, the export of these Hazaragi *kilims,* mostly from Sari-Pul, was limited. Business was in the hands of only one dealer, who exported about four to five thousand pieces to Jeddah every spring. In the mid-1970s, the production of these commercial *kilims* increased substantially. The main reasons for this were, firstly, the remittances sent home by thousands of Hazaras who had gone to Iran to work; secondly, three consecutive good harvest years; thirdly, an increased demand for Afghan goods in the Jeddah market (from where the majority of *kilims* go even further south to Yemen). Thus, the Hazaras were not forced to mortgage their wool to repay debts or to barter it for tea, sugar and other staples, and it was used to produce more items.

There are three main centres of commercial production of Hazaragi *kilims,* namely, Sari-Pul, Mazar-i-Sharif and Behsud.

Sari-Pul Production

Some forty-five kilometres south of Sheberghan lies the charming town of Sari-Pul, at the foothills of the northern folds of the Band-i-Turkestan range. Sari-Pul is an important *woleswali* serving a number of villages of diverse tribes which include Uzbek, Hazara, Pashtun and Aimaq. The Hazara of Sari-Pul originated from Uruzgan Province further south in the Hazarajat, from where they were forcibly moved and relocated by King Abdurahman in the late 1880s.

A high bridge over the Sari-Pul River welcomes one into this busy little town. The abundance of water is synonymous with fertility, and all around the town are stands of poplars and orchards of fruit trees. The streets are lined with trees, which give much needed shade in the burning heat of the summer. During harvest time, several large water mills steadily grind barley and wheat around the clock. In the spring, up and down the bazaar streets, men sit in front of little white piles of silkworm cocoons, for this region is also a centre of sericulture.

Sari-Pul is horse country, and although there are no Turkomans here, the traditional central Asian sport of *buzkashi,* and the Pashtun tent-pegging are practised by the Uzbek and Hazara. So it is not surprising to see, among the silversmiths who make adornments for the women of the different tribes, the carpenters who make wooden chests painted in bright colours, the saddlers at work on bridles, harnesses and stirrups, and the farriers and blacksmiths who

113

Colour Plate 113 HAZARA KILIM from Behsud. Note the predominance of orange and purple, which colours are so prevalent in this production, as is the use of dark undyed wool. The construction is much looser and flabbier than in either the Sari-Pul or Mazar productions, and the designs are both simpler and cruder. The Ghilzai wool in the warp ends (fringe) is very noticeable. (213 x 124cm).

Sari-Pul

Bamiyan valley

repair the carts and *gaadis.*

Bazaar days are Mondays and Thursdays, with Mondays the more important, especially for the marketing of the locally made *kilims*. Though traditionally woven by Hazaras, this craft is no longer their sole preserve, as today Uzbek and Pashtun are also weaving what is called the 'Hazaragi *kilim*', learned from the Hazaras. Several Sari-Pul merchants deal also in locally made *khourjeens* and nomad *torbahs,* brought in on bazaar days. One can also see some Turkoman-style rugs of abysmal quality, woven by local Uzbek. This production is still insignificant, but it is interesting that it has begun at all. Being sheep country, it may well develop. However, judging from experience, the Uzbek standard is never very high in those areas where there are no Turkomans for them to emulate.

The best *kilims* from this region are made in the large village of Charbagh, ten kilometres north of Sari-Pul on the road to Sheberghan, one of about twenty-five entirely Hazara villages around Sari-Pul. Charbagh numbers about five hundred and fifty houses, each of which has at least one loom. The various sized *kilims* are usually woven in pairs, using local spring-shorn Karaqul wool, mostly bought from Pashtun *maldars,* that is, animal owners. A 3½ x 1¼ metre *kilim,* one of a standard-sized pair, requires approximately 10½ kilos of wool, and can be woven by two women in six to seven days. As elsewhere in Afghanistan the looms, which are made from poplar wood, are horizontal.

While the wool and weave are of high quality, the same cannot be said of the dyestuffs, which are invariably the cheapest on the market and often fugitive. Blue, purple, orange, red, green and black are all used. The designs vary. The most popular is the *bagh-i-chinar* (poplar leaf), a series of serrated triangles in different colours often in the form of a diamond, and very different from the Turkoman design of the same name. New designs are being introduced continuously sometimes copies of the classical designs such as the Labijar *kheshti gul,* the Turkoman 'panel' design from Labijar, some fifty kilometres to the north. Others are garish and crude, and include flowers in a vase, reminiscent of those gaudy plastic bouquets sold in the Kabul bazaar. The traditional crenellated border is rapidly being replaced by the *lab-i-Mazar,* the Mazar border or lip, a small white motif woven into a black border.

Hazaragi *kilims* are also woven in some twenty-five other villages, inhabited mainly by Uzbek, Pashtun and Arabis. (See Colour Plate 112).

The Mazar Production

The production of Hazaragi *kilims* in the Mazar district varies little from that of Sari-Pul, and is made by Hazaras who have settled in and around the city, and in such villages as Urzgani, Chimtal, Sar-i-Asya and Imam Saheb. The Mazar *kilims* have the same tightness of weave as the Sari-Pul *kilims,* a similar range of sizes and designs, as well as colours and dyes used. They are sold in considerable quantities in the Mazar market, either retailed or dispatched by lorry to Kabul, where, in turn, they are sold in the Kabul *kilim* bazaar or exported to Jeddah.

The Behsud Production

Behsud, a small town perched on top of a hill in the heart of the Hazarajat, is another *woleswali* for a wide area of small villages situated in the valleys of this remote and near-barren mountain country. By and large, the Hazaragi *kilims* from Behsud and the surrounding areas are not of as good quality as those from Sari-Pul and Mazar. The majority of *kilims* woven for domestic use are made from Hazaragi wool, whereas those for the commercial market are generally made from Ghilzai wool, bought from the nomads who pass through with their flocks for summer grazing in the Hindi Kush.

The Behsud *kilims* are somewhat flabbier in texture than those from Sari-Pul and Mazar, but the colours used are similar and the designs, though often larger, follow much the same style and pattern. They are also usually woven in pairs, with perhaps a more frequent use of violet or purple, and orange stripes. (See Colour Plate 113).

One of the famous lakes of Band-i-Amir

Typical of the Hazarajat region

Colour Plate 114 *New Production (Afghanistan). A part-pile TAIMANI kilim being made in west central Afghanistan since about 1983. The designs of these pieces often include a stylised Tree of Life motif, flower vases and teapots. Another example of a new and commercial production despite the war. The flat weave is often embroidered with chain stitching. The piece shown is of a fairly common size, but smaller pieces are also being made. (265 x 158cm).*

Colour Plate 115 *New Production (Afghanistan). A part-pile TAIMANI prayer rug. This piece is typical of a new production which began around 1983. This rug was made in the Karokh district north of Herat City. Pieces of a similar appearance are also being made by the Mushwanis in Badghis Province. Both these productions are good examples of recent evolutionary trends in the Afghan carpet production, in spite of, and since, the war. (138 x 87cm).*

Chapter 14
Changes in the Carpet Industry within Afghanistan

The innate conservatism of the Turkomans has already been described earlier. It is, therefore, not surprising that during the period of 1979-1989 there has been little marked change in their carpet production — other than that caused by the direct and indirect effects of the war.

The number of weavers in Afghan Turkestan has been reduced by approximately 20% and, consequently, the meterage of Turkoman carpets exported directly from Kabul has slumped from a high of 17,250m^2 in 1979 to a low of 13,100m^2 in 1982/83, thereafter gradually increasing. In 1988 14,800m^2 were exported. Another factor affecting the Turkoman production was the sporadic and irregular availability of Karaqul wool. The flocks of Karaqul sheep have diminished by some 50% as a result of drought, reduced standards of animal husbandry and slaughter for food — both for the local population and for the occupying forces — as well as aerial strafing and deaths from mines. All these factors have meant that a proportion of Turkoman carpets was made with either poor quality Karaqul yarn or with other local yarns such as Hazaragi wool.

From 1980 to roughly 1985, Turkoman weavers were unwilling to make sizes larger than 3 x 2m^2. This reluctance was due to partly finished carpets still on the looms being slashed by vengeful Government soldiers searching for those young men who had joined the Mujahideen (Freedom Fighters). This lack of large carpet sizes was felt on the world wholesale markets. The author, who enjoys his own special production, was obliged to pay a premium for large sizes, thus underwriting the risks involved at that time. Yet, in spite of this, it was not until 1986 that he began to receive sizes of 2.5 x 3.5 metres.

In 1987, the Soviets, anxious to increase Afghan exports to the western markets and obtain the maximum of hard currency, instituted a fast and efficient road container service to London and other European destinations. Whilst this was a boon for the European and American wholesalers, it did not solve the Afghan exporters' problems. Carpets from the north and from Herat still had to be brought to Kabul for completion of customs' formalities and then be transported northwards again, where they were subjected to looting by the Mujahideen who would sell the rifled goods to finance the purchase of arms, medicines and other necessities. Soon a system of paying protection money was set up, forcing prices upwards. However, the demand for hard currency in Afghanistan in turn strengthened the free market rate for the U.S. dollar, thereby, to a large extent, offsetting increased costs in real terms and keeping prices at source in line with the western rates of inflation.

Until mid 1988, when military action around Jalalabad virtually closed the road, the official export of carpets and rugs from Afghanistan into Pakistan was via Torkham and through Peshawar. Practically all shops retailing rugs in Pakistan have on sale a significant number of Afghan goods. One wonders whether this extra exposure will effect favourably the future Afghan carpet production.

As would be expected, innovative changes which have taken place have been in those areas either totally under the control of Mujahideen field commanders or in cities firmly controlled by the Government.

Of these, Kabul is a good example. The 'Kabul production' — briefly mentioned on page 35 — has expanded considerably. What started as a new production in the mid-seventies can now be classed as a permanent addition to the carpet industry of Afghanistan. This totally non-traditional enterprise, using vertical looms in small ateliers, with male weavers from tribes having no carpet-weaving traditions — such as Hazaras, Tajiks and even some urbanised Pashtoons — has grown into a sizeable production. The pieces made here are of silk and depict a variety of designs, including classical Persian, Caucasian Kazak, stylised *purdah* (or Ensi) and *aski* (pictorial). The colours are muted and on the whole harmonious. Although the warps and pile are of silk, the wefts are cotton, resulting in a rather stiff handle and an untidy back. In this production can be included one or two ateliers run by established carpet exporters. Their products are fine, rather expensive and mostly made to order. To say more would give an unjustifiable bias to a production which is minute when considered in the general context of the Afghan carpet production.

The same can be said of the author's own production of fine Turkoman pieces, initiated in 1973 and totalling only some 80m² per month, the quality of which has improved markedly in recent years despite the war.

However, whilst there have indeed been changes and innovations during this period, they have mainly taken place within the Beluch-type production of western Afghanistan.

Beluch-type carpets and rugs

One innovation of interest is the 'war rug', first made in the area north-west of Herat City. These pieces featured, either in the field or in the border, such motifs as helicopters, tanks, bombs, airplanes, Kalashnikoffs, mines or explosive 'bursts'. It is known that the Beluch-type production often incorporates topical features in their weaving. So what could be more natural than to find the introduction of these elements in areas which had witnessed all the horrors of war?

A number of such pieces appeared on the market in the mid-eighties and were soon sold in Western markets, in the belief — no doubt enhanced by publicity in national newspapers — that 'war rugs' would become 'collectable items with a potential for long-term appreciation in value.'

This may be true as regards rugs made with quality yarn and superior workmanship. However, because of the large number of 'war rugs' being churned out in the Pakistani refugee camps (see chapter on refugee production in Pakistan) under the influence of misguided but entrepreneurial dealers and the use of poor materials and dyes, the author is sceptical about their long-term value.

The actual delineation between changes and innovations in the productions from within Afghanistan and from the Pakistan-based refugee camps is difficult to pinpoint. Because of the communications network and the constant to-ing and fro-ing of Afghan Mujahideen, at one time there was a good deal of copying and, therefore, overlapping of the two productions. But the deciding and prominent factor in the difference between the two productions is the quality of the yarn used in any given piece, rather than the standard of workmanship, and in this the production within Afghanistan is favoured.

A good example of quality pieces coming out of Afghanistan is the part-pile Taimani and Mushwani production of prayer rugs and *dasterkhans* (see Colour Plates 114, 115, 116, 117). The Taimani production is mainly from the area east of Herat to the western limits of Hazarajat; the Mushwani production is from the west and north of Herat — Ghorian, Karokh. These pieces are now found in the bazaars of Peshawar, Lahore, Islamabad, Quetta and Karachi where they are sold to foreign dealers at a handsome profit.

From the same areas in Afghanistan as mentioned above, there has been a noticeable increase in the production of square part-pile *dasterkhans,* as well as *kilim dasterkhans.* Additionally, the Mushwanis have been making very colourful and intricate *dasterkhans* — some of which are considerably longer than the standard two metres, going up to four metres in length. Of intricate design, the colouring of these pieces usually includes 'old gold' and all other typical Mushwani attributes. However, this is a new and commercial production.

Late in 1983, the first part-pile Taimani *kilims* (see Colour Plate ?) began to appear. Most of these pieces are made in sizes of approximately 240 x 140cm, though smaller pieces are also made. The flat-woven area is usually covered with chain stitching in white, whilst the piled areas are generally of indigo, a deep maroon-red and purple, this latter colour being obtained by the mixing of indigo and red. Common to all productions, the standard of workmanship varies from good to poor, as do the designs. Frequently seen in the central panel is a knotted and piled stylised Tree of Life on a white field. Border designs often feature teapots, flower vases, large rosettes (new) and/or the traditional Taimani star motif. Whilst this production is by no means vast, it is distinctive and generally well made.

Some three years later, in 1987, another Beluch-type production, largely made up by the Farsi-speaking Latif Khol tribe from the south of Herat City and the Adraskhan region, began to appear. These pieces, seldom larger than 150 x 90cm, comprise a central squarish piled area running the width of the rug and for a similar length. At either ends are *kilims* measuring some 30cm which are patterned with stripes and often having tassels. The designs of the piled areas are too numerous to describe, but the colouring is usually sombre, with mauvish blues, deep and dark reds lightened with white.

Thus we see in the space of a decade the introduction of four new types of rugs from Afghanistan, and this despite the war. In the previous decade, there were only two new productions, that of the Tchitchaktus in the north and the Kabul atelier pieces.

An unexplained phenomenon has been the appearance of both Persian and Turkish goods offered for sale in the Kabul bazaar since late 1987. Old Turkish *kilim* bedrolls and cradles as well as new *kilims* have been available sporadically at prices less than those appertaining in the country of origin. Also, Kurdish flat-woven bags and *kilims* from Quchan, as well as piled and flat weaves from various parts of Iran have been available in modest quantities, and irregularly. Less surprisingly, fine Persian Mashad Beluch prayer rugs and fine Beluch-type pieces made by Afghan refugees in Iran have also found their way to the Kabul bazaar. The refugee production boasts excellent colour combinations and good geometric designs, though not strictly traditional ones.

One wonders what impact these trends, coupled with those changes which have occurred in the Afghan refugee production from Pakistan, will have on the future of the Afghan carpet industry.

It seems highly probable that in another ten years this book will again have to be revised!

116

117

Colour Plate 116 *New production (Afghanistan). A part-pile MUSHWANI prayer rug from the Karokh region north of Herat City, depicting a new design. This production started circa 1984. (107 x 80cm).*

Colour Plate 117 *New production (Afghanistan). An example of the changes in the MUSHWANI production. This piled prayer rug made in the Karokh region north of Herat City has a 10cm-long kilim at both ends. Note the incidence of 'old gold', which is a feature of the Mushwanis from the north-west of Afghanistan. (103 x 80cm).*

118

Colour Plate 118 New
production (Afghanistan). A
stylised BESHIR BOTEH design
woven in Qala-i-Zal in Kunduz
Province, with hand-spun
Karaqul yarn that has been dyed
with natural dyestuffs.
146 x 99cm).

Chapter 15
Afghan Refugees Pakistan

By far the largest concentration of the three million Afghan refugees in Pakistan is in the North West Frontier Province (NWFP), which has a common border with the eastern provinces of Afghanistan. Most of the refugees in the NWFP are Pashtu-speakers, in whose culture carpet weaving has virtually no place. There are, however, also large numbers of refugees from the north of Afghanistan, mainly Turkomans and some Uzbeks, for whom carpet weaving is very much a tradition and way of life. The refugee camps of Beluchistan also house a significant number of Turkomans, Uzbeks and other carpet-weaving tribal groups from northern Afghanistan.

In order to better understand and appreciate the remarkable developments in the Afghan carpet production within the refugee camps that have taken place during the decade since the Soviet invasion, one must remember the utter misery and deprivation experienced by these unhappy people. They arrived, the old, the young and the very young, bringing with them the few personal possessions they could carry. They were allocated tented accommodation — anathema to those who had always lived in walled compounds which embraced the ageless and innate security derived from the extended family system, at the same time ensuring the protection and privacy of their womenfolk. They were kept alive through humanitarian aid from the UNHCR, the UN and countless other assistance programmes from countries around the world and especially through the Government of Pakistan which has sustained the largest refugee population in history.

As far as possible, the refugees tried to recreate their former ways of life, a mammoth task calling for unending courage, for those with no income, minimal possessions, living at subsistence level, for the bereaved — all experiencing the soul-destroying anguish of an uncertain future, compounded by grief and boredom.

Among the approximately eighty foreign relief agencies in Pakistan working for the Afghan refugee communities, a few are involved in different income-generating projects related to carpet weaving. These activities, when considering the Afghan carpet production as a whole, are probably of little significance. But, alas, this laudable concept has often been pursued by well-intentioned folk with no regard whatsoever for the culture and traditions of peoples of widely differing roots. In my opinion, some of these efforts are terribly misguided, and it is little wonder that they face marketing problems when, for instance, computer-made designs in unpallatable colour combinations without one iota of Afghan cultural symbols are given to weavers for copying in hand-knotted rugs. Likewise, I have seen geometric designs in hideous colours, which would shame the least skilled designer of the cheapest linoleums. One such agency found that rugs made by their own trained Pashtun weavers, bearing such slogans as 'Happy Birthday, Uncle George' did not sell readily; they are now making quasi-traditional Turkoman designs, the centre of the *guls* containing such logos as IBM and BoA (Bank of America)! What an unintentional insult; what wasted opportunities and resources! Happily, I do not think that this type of tasteless production is likely to be perpetuated. The West certainly has a great deal to re-learn from the East!

The Government of Pakistan, through its department for the promotion of small industries instituted a programme in the early eighties to train young boys from some of the refugee camps in carpet making. These boys — all Pashtuns — were taught to make typical Pakistani rugs on vertical looms in several small training centres located in Peshawar and around the N.W.F.P. For budgetary reasons this scheme was abandoned in 1987.

Yet another example of teaching carpet weaving in refugee camps was encountered in a camp situated north of Quetta in Baluchistan. Here, under the tutelage of a Turkoman male, some thirty boys from Kandahar were busily weaving carpets of varying designs on horizontal looms. The author was surprised to see a Persian Mir-Serabend with a mustard-coloured ground being made next to a classical Turkoman Bashiri, and further on down the line a Samarkand on loom next to a Tabriz. In this workshop, which produces carpets on special orders from Western buyers, the standard of workmanship was impressive. Thus, it must be recognised that during the past decade a number of non-traditional weavers has been introduced to the craft of carpet making — albeit with wide-ranging emphasis. It remains to be seen to what extent these trends will be manifested in the future Afghan production.

Another and welcome development of far greater importance has been the very marked improvement in both design and quality, as well as colour harmony, in rugs made by Pashtun and Uzbek refugees who had come from Baghlan Province. As mentioned earlier, Amir Abdul Rahman, in the late 1880s, forcibly dispersed large groups of Pashtuns to the north of Afghanistan (see page 157) in an attempt to unify the country through a policy of 'divide and rule'. Some of these Pashtuns were settled in Baghlan Province, which lies south of Kunduz and east of Samangan, and they slowly learned the skill from their carpet-making neighbours.

Their pre-war production, mainly cheap and characterless *boleshts,* piled prayer rugs and also kilim prayer rugs, all of which were marketed through Kunduz, was considered of insufficient importance to merit mention in the first edition of this book. However, the current 'Baghlani' production, mostly from refugee camps in the N.W.F.P., is well-made, being of above average density for this Baluch-type production. In addition, both designs and colour harmony are well suited to the Western taste. Most pieces are of rug sizes, but carpet sales are also made, including some with new non-traditional designs being produced by Turkomans. These two productions, however, cannot be confused, as the Baghlani weave is closer in all respects to the Tchitchaktu and other Beluch-type goods. The range of Baghlani designs is too wide to enumerate here; they include both traditionally based designs and a range of *narche gashtai* (literally, 'wandering design'). Unfortunately, the use of local mill-spun yarn, whilst it reacts favourably to the Pakistani chemical wash to which all Pakistani carpets are subjected, does, involve a degree of wool shedding.

Yet another new venture is the Baghlani production of flat weaves. In this, they have not been inventive, preferring to copy already existing productions. The author has seen fair imitations of the Dali *kilim* (see Colour Plate 51), though somewhat coarser than the original. This may have been due to the yarn used. Likewise, Larghabi *kilims,* an Uzbek sumak-type construction, in small and large sizes are being made. Also being made are very good copies of the Moghur Beluch kilims, a heavy and somewhat coarser fabric, in the construction of which the floating weft is much used. These are woven in all sizes, the majority of which are sold abroad.

Dyestuffs are another problem. On his most recent visit to one of the long-established refugee camps in July, 1989, the author heard many complaints from Turkoman weavers concerning the quality of currently available

119

120

Colour Plate 119 Refugee production (Pakistan). A typical example of a narche jangi *'war rug' being made in refugee camps of the N.W.F.P. in Pakistan. These pieces are often made by children, both Turkoman and Uzbek, as qualifying tests of their weaving skills. Note the cotton warps — a cheaper material than wool. Also the range of warfaring items: a Kalashnikov machine gun, tanks, grenades, bombs and mines. (94 x 51cm).*

Colour Plate 120 Refugee Turkoman production (Pakistan). An example of a non-traditional NARCHE GASHTAI design, woven by Turkoman refugees in Pakistan with local mill-spun yarn dyed with synthetic dyestuffs. The runner shown has a dark blue field but similar pieces also have a field of deep cherry-red. This production began in 1984 and is proving popular. (250 x 82cm).

121

*Colour Plate 121 Refugee Turkoman production (Pakistan). A classical Beshiri ALMA GUL design, made in the North West Frontier Province refugee camps by Turkoman refugees using local mill-spun yarn dyed with local synthetic dyestuffs.
182 x 124cm).*

dyestuffs. In the camps, local dyes, as well as dyes imported from such countries as Rumania, China and Germany were on sale. Certainly, some dyestuffs used in the Afghan refugee production are fugitive, and, regrettably, circumstances did not allow further investigation into those frequent complaints regarding poor and unsatisfactory results after dyeing the yarn. Bearing in mind that the refugees dye their yarn in open vats rather than in pressure vats, it was impossible to apportion the blame to the dyestuffs, the quality of the yarn or the dyeing process! Suffice it to say that the craftsmen themselves were dissatisfied, and also that most complaints came from those using the poorer quality yarns.

It must be emphasised here that local Pakistani mill-spun yarn, of whatever quality, cannot be equated with healthy Afghan hand-spun Karaqul yarn, the wearing qualities and natural lustre of which are difficult to match. The wool mills in Pakistan produce a range of qualities, varying in long staple content, lustre and colour, which, of course, has a direct bearing on tones after dyeing. Colours range from white to ivory, cream to almost yellow; the degree of lustre varies from an acceptable standard to an almost opaque, dry and harsh yarn, down to recycled wool spun from second-hand clothing containing a proportion of man-made fibres. The top quality and most expensive yarn is imported from Australia and is referred to locally as 'Merino', a good blended yarn, white and lustrous.

In the beginning of the period under consideration, refugees, particularly those of the Turkoman tribes, made carpets with yarn of Karaqul wool which they had brought with them or had sent to them from Afghanistan. In addition, a number of refugees had brought with them small flocks of Karaqul sheep which by 1988 had virtually died out. The Turkoman weavers, therefore, had to resort to the use of local yarn. Those skilled weavers who could afford the imported yarn, or the best of the local yarns, were in the minority. There is no doubt that the insecurities of their life as refugees, the uncertainty of sales, the natural reluctance to spend capital on the more expensive materials — including dyestuffs — were all understandable reasons for the production of poor-quality goods. Market forces prevailed, and when it was realised that this inexpensive and sub-standard production did not readily sell, the Turkomans soon changed their strategy.

Herein lies the main reason for some of the most marked changes in the refugee production. By the middle of 1989, those Turkomans who had resisted making carpets with non-traditional designs were producing, in appreciable quantities, pieces with Turkoman motifs which had been abandoned since the 1960s. Among these are the Sulayman *fil-pai* encased in panels, the basic colours highlighted with dark green; both the Beshiri *alma gul* and *boteh;* the Akhel *gul;* the *kheshti gul,* and some of the older variations of the Ersari Chobash. Included also are the whole range of *fil-pai* motifs and the Keldar *purdah* (some of these on silk warps!) and, of course, some *kar-i-safide.* It would seem that the current Turkoman production — at the time of writing — comprises some 70-80% of traditional designs, supplemented by 20-30% of *narche gashtai.*

Some of the Tekke Turkomans from Barmazid are now producing very fine and attractive Kizilayak 'mosque' prayer rugs. These pieces are on silk warps and contain some silk motifs. While they are not exact replicas — the field is generally dark blue — they are finer than the genuine Barmazid production of pre-1979.

In addition, Turkomans and some Uzbeks are now making *narche gashtai* (new non-traditional) designs and even copying some of the fine Persian origins. This production would appear to be 20-30%. The author was surprised to see copies of the Tabriz Herati design in sizes of 6m² and of 240 x 150cm also. While these pieces were of significantly coarser stitch than the Persian Tabriz, the motifs were, nonetheless, outlined in silk. In most of these fine carpets, imported yarn was used; local yarn is used for the poorer qualities. The use of cotton warps in refugee camps is not, alas, confined to the poorer qualities alone.

A number of small mats can also be found. These are coarse in structure, with the pile of very poor quality local yarn knotted on cotton warps and depicting crude 'war designs' (*narche jangi*). These pieces, I am told, are made by Turkoman and Uzbek children — a sort of 'passing out' test — and have replaced the small Aq Chah mats which were a common feature of the Kabul bazaar in pre-war days.

Lastly should be mentioned the definite increase in the number of male weavers, both among the Turkomans and other tribes. Undoubtedly, this is largely due to the lack of occupational activities available in camp life.

Carpets and rugs made in Pakistan for export have, by law, to be handled by a Pakistani exporter in possession of a *Jawaz Tejerati* (trade licence). Thus no Afghan, nor indeed anyone else, can export goods in his own name. This means that the monopoly of the Afghan refugee production is entirely in the hands of established Pakistani exporters/wholesalers, who soon acquainted themselves with the needs of such world markets as Hamburg, London and New York. This, in turn, must influence the Afghan refugee production to some extent.

Turkey

In 1981, the Turkish Government granted asylum to some 4,000 Afghans of Turkic origin, mainly Turkomans, Uzbeks and Khirgiz. This humane act has perhaps not received the recognition that it merits.

The families in question enjoyed common religious, cultural, linguistic and ancestral roots with their hosts, thus minimising the risk of these refugees becoming an unwelcome minority, whilst at the same time maximising the chances of a quicker and less painful assimilation. They were given housing and land, as well as an initial allowance sufficient for them to begin to develop income-related occupations of their choosing.

The refugees were divided into small groups, consideration being given to their tribal, clan and family associations, thereby setting the scene for the recreation of village communal life which is so much part of their heritage and culture. These communities were sited in four main regions of Turkey, the most important being in Tokat Province north of Sivas and in Van in eastern Turkey.

By no means were all of these people traditional carpet weavers. The Kirghiz, who left their homeland in the Pamirs as early as 1979 and are now settled in the Van district, had abandoned weaving several decades ago. They are now engaged in agriculture and pastoral activities, supplemented by petty trading. It is to be hoped that they can be encouraged to recommence their traditional craft of making *torbahs*, rugs and other tent furnishings, which are so distinctive and typical.

122

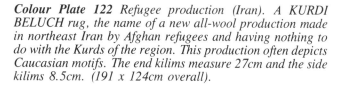

123

124

Colour Plate 122 *Refugee production (Iran). A KURDI BELUCH rug, the name of a new all-wool production made in northeast Iran by Afghan refugees and having nothing to do with the Kurds of the region. This production often depicts Caucasian motifs. The end kilims measure 27cm and the side kilims 8.5cm. (191 x 124cm overall).*

Colour Plate 123 *Refugee production (Iran). A very finely woven part-pile Beluch-type kilim made by Afghan refugees in the Mashad district of northeast Iran. The central cross and wide border, which measures 20cm and features the* aina gul *motif, are knotted and piled. (183 x 107cm).*

Colour Plate 124 *Refugee production (Iran). A KURDI BELUCH prayer rug, strongly reminiscent of the Caucasian Shirvan* marasai. *Made entirely of wool with a fine stitch, this piece is another example of the Afghan refugee production in Iran. (151 x 101cm).*

Likewise, many of the Uzbeks now in Turkey have no weaving tradition. Of the relatively few who lived in close proximity to the Turkomans of northern Afghanistan, only a handful is now making rugs or carpets. They prefer such occupations as the making of leather garments, the manufacture of metal utensils, and trading, all of which bring in a more regular and assured income with no capital outlay.

In the Tokat region where many, if not most, of the Turkomans mainly from Sheberghan, are now settled, the pattern is similar, it is from here, however, that the majority of the Turkoman carpets originate. The production is not large and, to date, it is still traditional, superficially at least, that is, the pieces are of wool warps and wefts, the designs are *fil-pai* or Bokhara *kar-i-sefide,* and they are knotted on horizontal looms, unlike the vast majority of Turkish carpets which are not made on vertical looms. In colouring there is a tendency towards the non-traditional, with a penchant for fields of gold, cream and even green. The wool, being softer than the traditional Karaqul yarn, results in a very different handle of the finished pieces, and responds more readily to a light chemical wash.

Whilst this production is found in limited quantities in the carpet shops that proliferate in and around the Istanbul bazaar, it is far too early to comment reliably on either the wearing qualities or the popularity of this production. One thing is certain, however. To whatever extent the Turkish carpet production, now undergoing marked evolutionary changes, may have gained from the influx of Afghan Turkoman weavers, the Afghan production has lost accordingly.

Iran

The author, holder of a British passport, had hoped to visit Iran during May, 1989, but he was refused a visa. The difficulties in collating and verifying information on the carpet production of Afghan refugees in Iran will, therefore, be readily appreciated.

The majority of the two million Afghan refugees in Iran are concentrated in and around Meshed, the capital of Khorassan Province in the north-east of the country. They are mainly Dari (Persian)-speakers and Sunni Moslems.

Whilst most of the Turkoman refugees are in Pakistan, some went to Iran, where they are dispersed in comparatively small groups in the north-east of the country, not far from the Soviet Republic of Turkmenistan, from where their forebears fled from the Bolshevik suppression of 1921 and onwards. Other Iranian Turkoman communities, mainly Yamouds and Tekkes, came from Ashkabad also in the early 1920s and settled in and around Gombad-i-Qabus.

The Afghan Turkoman refugees are currently making carpets mainly depicting the *fil-pai* motif, and their production is absorbed into that of the Iranian Turkomans. The Iranian Turkoman production, the construction of which differs markedly from the Afghan, is woven with cotton warps and seldom portrays the *fil-pai.* It will be interesting to see whether the Afghan Turkomans retain the integrity of their traditions.

In the Beluch and Beluch-type production of an estimated 5,000 Afghan refugee weavers, there are some interesting developments. A new production, locally called 'Kurdi Quchans' began to appear around 1985-86. Both the construction and designs of these pieces are very different from the well-known Quchan production. It was at first thought that this was an example of evolutionary change in the industry — similar to many currently taking place in Turkey. However, it was established that these pieces were being made by Afghan refugees!

In addition, some very fine pieces, copies of old Persian and Caucasian rugs are now appearing on the market. Some of these pieces have found their way to the Kabul bazaar, where they have been bought on behalf of the author. Others have been smuggled into Pakistan. This production, still somewhat limited, is often of extreme fineness and exact colour reproduction, and is made under the supervision and tutelage of Iranian master weavers.

A few of these Afghan weavers have attained such a degree of skill as to be able to break away from the atelier and start on their own. Indeed, the author knows of one such weaver who has been induced to come to Pakistan, there to weave for his mentor, an Afghan refugee from Herat.

Thus, we see here another example of change in the carpet industry. To date, these productions are all exported from Iran as Persian goods; what will happen when these skilled Afghan refugees return to their own country?

Glossary
The Carpets of Afghanistan

Afs. short for Afghanis, the Afghan currency

Aimaq Mongolian word meaning nomad

akhel gul shape of gul attributed to the region of Akhel in Soviet Turkestan, larger than the Tekke gul

alma gul apple blossom motif

alum (zantch) a chemical used as a mordant in dyeing woollen yarn

Arabi breed of sheep, also tribe — lit. 'from Arab'

ashqar peganum harmala which when charred is used as a mordant in the dyeing of indigo and madder

asmalyk a Turkoman 5-sided piled (sometimes felt) fabric, piece often used to decorate the flanks of either camels or horses

badam gul almond blossom motif, sometimes described as the man with two wives

bagh-i-shinar gul the poplar leaf design

bastani gul (gul-i-bastani) the 'closed' or enclosed design

Beluch a tribe

Beluchi a breed of sheep; a fat tailed variety, lit. of the Beluch

Bokhara gul Bokhara design = Tekke gul or design

bolesht (or pushti) a tent bag whose opening is at the narrow end varying in size and shape, also used as cushions or pillows

boteh a design motif of unknown origin, though probably Chinese, much used by crafts- men in the reign of Shah Abbas, and latterly called in England the 'Paisley' design

buzkashi lit. 'pulling the goat' — a Turkoman sport played on horseback

camel hair sometimes used in the weaving of rugs, especially in the border guards

candlestick motif a motif suggesting a multiple candlestick, typically used in purdahs

cat's foot a recurring very small squarish gul in the Cherqchi production

Caucasian design narche kafqazi

chaikhana tea house or inn

chapan the long sleeved coat, often of brightly coloured silk or artificial silk worn by Turkomans and some Uzbeks

chapari the rounded felt tent similar to the yurt, but smaller and generally lower, used by various transhumants

char or chahar means four, hence Char Aimaqs = the Four Aimaqs

charpai a bed, the frame of which is made of wood, often poplar, and which is interlaced with a type of rush/reed

chodor gul a flattened diamond pattern containing nine small motifs — a type of gul attributed to the Chodors. Whilst there are no Chodors in Afghanistan, this gul is used especially in purdahs

choval *see* juwal

chowkidar watchman (chowki = chair)

Christmas tree design or inverted ribcage motif

dallal — a broker

dasterkhan — a tablecloth or eating cloth

Dokhtar-i-Qazi — a design often seen in Beluch-type prayer rugs; lit. 'the Judge's daughter'

eating cloth — *see* dasterkhan

eight flower motif — the secondary gul used in various Turkoman carpet designs — (gul-i-gul)

elephant's foot — *see* fil-pai

ensi or engsi (USSR) — meaning the design used on yurt closures. Not used in Afghanistan (see hatchlu and purdah).

fil-pai gul — lit. 'elephant's foot', the largest Ersari gul or design which varies according to the clan

flat weave — *see* kilim

gaadi — two wheeled horse-drawn vehicle used as a taxi in the provinces

Gaadic — a breed of sheep, the wool from which is used in Beluch carpets

gaz — a cradle (see salanchak), also the name given to a 1,500 kilo Russian-made lorry

ghajari — a term used by Turkomans for all lightweight tapestry weaves

Ghilzai — nomad breed of sheep found mainly in the Hindu Kush and Hazarajat mountains; a fat tailed species

Ghiordes knot — (Turkish knot) rarely used in Afghan carpets

gilam — dialect and dialectical pronounciation of kilim

grut — hard sun dried lumps of soured milk curds, the staple diet of nomadic shepherds

gul — flower or motif/design

gul donneh or gul donni — the flower vase motif, or flowered pieces, applies to namads

gul-i-gul — lit. the flower of flowers. An Ersari and Turkoman gul

gul-i-namad — the flowered namad i.e. a namad with a flowered motif

Haft Bolah — means Seven Up or Seven Demons, — a small Pushtu speaking tribe; also the name of a rug design

hatchlu (Iran) — *see* ensi, engsi, and purdah

Hazaragi — breed of sheep native to the central mountains of the Hazarajat, lit. of Hazaras

Herati — breed of sheep found mainly in the Herat area, lit. of Herat

hessian — jute — or sacking made from jute fibres

horizontal loom — the most basic type of loom, used by nomadic weavers and Turkomans

ikat — the Uzbek technique of binding material (usually silk) so that patches of fibres will not be exposed to the dye, and repeating the process so that a pattern of different colours results

indigo — a natural or synthetic dyestuff

inverted ribcage — Christmas tree design

isparak also sparak — a plant producing a bright yellow natural dyestuff

jallar — a tent bag, having width exceeding height

jallar paidar — a jallar with 'feet', hence used over doors and doorways

jangal — wood or forest

Judge's daughter — *see* Dokhtar-i-Qazi

juwal/juval/choval — the largest of the tent bags, often referred to as camel bags

juwal gul — the most frequently reproduced design used on juwals

Kandahari — a breed of sheep from the semi-desert regions around Kandahar

karachi — a two wheeled flat cart used in towns for transporting loads, and generally pushed and/or pulled by men

Karaqul — a breed of sheep indigenous to

Uzbekistan in the Soviet Union and the north of Afghanistan, which has a dual fleece and which provides an excellent wool for carpets

kar-i-sefide — lit. 'white work', i.e. designs containing white, especially the Bokhara pattern

kari-i-surkh — lit. 'red work', i.e. designs in which there is no white, — nearly all 'elephant's foot' designs

kemp — the name for the coarse rough hairs found in a fleece

kermes — (from the Arabic qirmiz = crimson) the dried bodies of insects found in oak bark, used as a dyestuff

khariji — foreigner

khesht — a brick

kheshti gul — brick design i.e. a rectangular motif

khourjeen — a double bag which can be either knotted and piled or flat woven. Frequently misnamed a 'donkey bag'

kilim — flat weaving without raised texture or nap; kilims are often long and narrow, woven in one piece or in two or more bands later sewn together. A carpet starts and ends in a kilim — a band of flat weave

kleenah — driver's apprentice who also cleans the vehicle

knee-caps — worn by camels or horses, they are often knotted and piled and with small bells attached

kola — the skull cap around which the males wear a turban, and over which women place a veil

kola-i-chergh — kilim bags made in pairs for keeping together the ends of the yurt poles when the caravan is on the move

kuchi — a perjorative word for nomads which means gypsy

Lab-i-Mazar — the Mazar border or lip, a small white motif woven into a black border

madder (royan) — a natural dyestuff obtained from the roots of the madder bush, which produces warm mellow reds, varying in shade according to the thickness and age of the root stem

mafraj — a small tent bag often used by women to store their personal belongings

maldar — a flock owner, a wealthy man

Marco Polo sheep — sheep found in the Wakhan Corridor and Pamir Mountains on the borders with China

masjid — mosque

Masjid-i-Gombad — the mosque with nine domes, a 10th century ruin at Balkh

mast — yoghurt

Mauri — now a quality rug woven in and around Herat by Turkomans, and marketed there. Originally a word coined to describe those Turkomans who came from Merv, and includes Yamouds, Tekkes and Saruqs

mehman — a guest

mehman-khanah — a guest house or guest room

mihrab — the niche inside the mosque which always faces towards Mecca, and is a main feature of prayer rugs

money bag — *see* pul donneh

mordant — any substance that combines with and fixes a dyestuff in material that cannot be dyed direct

mullah — a Muslim religious leader

namad — a felt, traditionally made from the autumn clip, which can be used as floor coverings, or sheets for yurts

namak donneh — salt bag, is a small torbah, nearly always flat woven

narche — a picture or drawing

narche gashtai — lit. a 'wandering design', thus a non-traditional one which has no name, no family clan or tribal origin

narche kafqazi — Caucasian design

naswar	ground tobacco, which in Afghanistan is frequently used as an oral snuff
Nau Rouz	lit. New Day. New Year, the 21st March and Spring Equinox, which was in being in the time of Zoroaster prior to the Islamic conversion
neck-band	a band worn by a camel or donkey, to which is attached a bell, — a type of halter
nockle	a sugar coated almond nut or chickpea through which tea is drunk
nomad	one of a wandering pastoral community
Paisley design	*see* boteh
panj	five
panj mihrabha	five mihrabs, name of a design used in the Tchitchaktu production
peganum harmala	*see* ashqar
Persian knot (or Senneh knot)	an asymmetric knot used in all Afghan carpets
pillau	a rice dish cooked with much fat, which contains a lump of meat in the centre
pine tree motif	another term for inverted ribcage motif
pul donneh (or pul donni)	a purse, or money bag
purdah (curtain)	(*see* ensi, hatchlu) either the design or the woven piece which used to serve as the inside closure of the yurt
qaqmai torbah	flat woven tent bag
qazi	a judge
qirmiz	*see* kermes
royan	madder
runner	long, narrow carpet
running dog motif	a motif used by the Saltuqs and others
saddle cloth	zin-i-asp
sadranji	a cotton flat woven fabric. In India and Pakistan called dhurrie
safidi qandi	hypochlorite bleach, (used to bleach sugar), which when mixed with water produces chlorine
sag-i-ramah	the guard dogs used by the nomads to guard their flocks
salanchak	a cradle, a woven piece, sometimes called a gaz
Salor gul	a motif used by the Salors in their rug making
salt bag	namak donneh or donni
samovar	tea house (*see* chaikhana) also urn used for boiling water
sarhad	border or frontier
seer	a measure of weight which varies with the locality; in Afghan Turkestan, a seer is equivalent to seven kilos
seh	three
seh mihrabha	three mihrabs
serai	a courtyard in which animals are tethered, and around which are rooms for lodging and storage purposes, also an open space for caravans to load or unload goods; abbreviation of caravanserai
seven demons and seven up	*see* Haft Bolah
shaali	from the Persian shal — shawl; given to the shepherd by each owner at the end of the season, this he may sell, or make into a shawl or coat
sparak	*see* isparak
star motif	a symbol with strong Taghan associations and found in Taimani production
Sygyrnme design	the motif at the skirt or end of some Turkoman rugs
tapestry weave	simplest form of flat weaving technique
taqir	the unborn lamb from the Karaqul sheep (Persian lamb)
tar	thread, warp
tea house	*see* chaikhana

tent-band	used inside and outside the yurt, to provide both decoration and a support to which tent bags may be attached
torbah	a tent bag, sometimes placed on the back of the camel by nomads when the clan is on the move
toshak	a thin cotton filled mattress or palliasse
tree motif	peculiar to the Taghan, Dali, Qarqeen and Old Sulayman production
Tree of Life design	a tree or plant motif used in various forms
trefoil motif	a motif suggesting a trefoil or clover leaf, used in most Ersari elephant's foot guls
Turkoman	a member of a large ethnic group, the majority of whom live in USSR, but some who sought refuge now live in Iran and Afghanistan

wandering design	*see* narche gashtai
wazir	minister
woleswali	an administrative area/district
yak-o-neem tara	lit. one and a half threads i.e. a thick weft followed by a thinner one
Yaqub Khana	lit. Jacob's House, name of a Beluch design, and of a Persian speaking tribe
yurt	traditional circular domed wood framed tent made of felt, used by nomads
zahr-i-choub	'yellow wood', *see* isparak
zantch	alum
zin-i-asp	saddle cloth
zir-i-pai	lit. under foot — 'used' — applies to a piece which has lost the newness associated with pieces straight off the loom

INDEX

Books on Textiles from the

Antique Collectors' Club

5 Church Street, Woodbridge, Suffolk, England
Tel: Woodbridge (0394) 385501. Fax. No. (03943) 4434

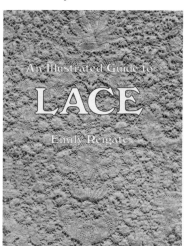

Ian Bennett

Oriental Rugs: Caucasian *by Ian Bennett* 10 x 8½in. 376 pp., 155 b. & w. illus., 336 col. ISBN 0 902028 58 8. The large number of colour illustrations enables the author to show both the wide range of quality and the various types available on the market today. This is generally accepted as the most useful book on the subject.

Oriental Rugs: Persian *by Erich Aschenbrenner* 10 x 8½in. 272 pp., 141 col. illus. ISBN 0 907462 12 X. Describes each area of manufacture divided into towns and villages whose rugs display individual characteristics. As the quality of rugs varies considerably, this book serves as a good, general introduction to the subject.

Oriental Rugs: Turkish *by C. Fritzsche and K. Zipper* 10 x 8½in. 260pp. 275 col. illus. ISBN 1 85149 091 4. The Ottoman Empire dominated Eastern Europe for five hundred years, output was vast and exported worldwide. Lavish colour and the author's factual comments make this an invaluable book.

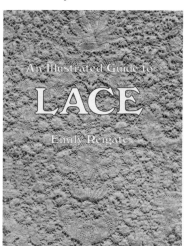

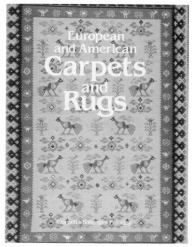

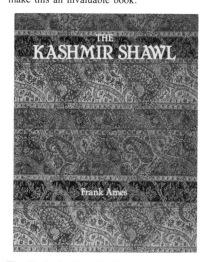

An Illustrated Guide to Lace *by Emily Reigate* 264 pp., 700 b. & w. illus., 12 col. ISBN 1 85149 003 5. An incomparable collection of photographs of lace from the great centres of lacemaking in Italy, France, Flanders and England. Each example is placed in its geographical and historical context from the 17th century to the present day.

European and American Carpets and Rugs *by Cornelia Bateman Faraday* 464pp., 326 b. & w. illus., 103 col. ISBN 1 85149 092 2. This fascinating and contemporary account, with additional modern colour, covers American, Austrian, Belgian, British, Dutch, East European, French, German, Italian, Scandinavian and Spanish carpets and rugs.

The Kashmir Shawl *by Frank Ames* 352 pp., 262 b. & w. illus., 86 col., 33 line drawings. ISBN 1 85149 079 5. The first detailed account of the evolution, structure, fabrication and symbolism of this fascinating branch of textiles, now in a revised edition.

THE ANTIQUE COLLECTORS' CLUB

The Antique Collectors' Club was formed in 1966 and now has a five figure membership spread throughout the world. It publishes the only independently run monthly antiques magazine *Antique Collecting* which caters for those collectors who are interested in widening their knowledge of antiques, both by greater awareness of quality and by discussion of the factors which influence the price that is likely to be asked. The Antique Collectors' Club pioneered the provision of information on prices for collectors and the magazine still leads in the provision of detailed articles on a variety of subjects.

It was in response to the enormous demand for information on ''what to pay'' that the price guide series was introduced in 1968 with the first edition of *The Price Guide to Antique Furniture* (completely revised, 1978 and 1989), a book which broke new ground by illustrating the more common types of antique furniture, the sort that collectors could buy in shops and at auctions rather than the rare museum pieces which had previously been used (and still to a large extent are used) to make up the limited amount of illustrations in books published by commercial publishers. Many other price guides have followed, all copiously illustrated, and greatly appreciated by collectors for the valuable information they contain, quite apart from prices. The Antique Collectors' Club also publishes other books on antiques, including horology and art reference works, and a full book list is available.

Club membership, which is open to all collectors, costs £17.50 per annum. Members receive free of charge *Antique Collecting,* the Club's magazine (published ten times a year), which contains well-illustrated articles dealing with the practical aspects of collecting not normally dealt with by magazines. Prices, features of value, investment potential, fakes and forgeries are all given prominence in the magazine.

Among other facilities available to members are private buying and selling facilities, the longest list of ''For Sales'' of any antiques magazine, an annual ceramics conference and the opportunity to meet other collectors at their local antique collectors' clubs. There are over eighty in Britain and more than a dozen overseas. Members may also buy the Club's publications at special pre-publication prices.

As its motto implies, the Club is an amateur organisation designed to help collectors get the most out of their hobby: it is informal and friendly and gives enormous enjoyment to all concerned.

For Collectors — By Collectors — About Collecting

The Antique Collectors' Club, 5 Church Street, Woodbridge, Suffolk
Tel: Woodbridge (0394) 385501. Fax No. (03943) 4434